Discovery and Disclosure Practice, Problems, and Proposals for Change:

A Case-based National Survey of Counsel in Closed Federal Civil Cases

Thomas E. Willging, John Shapard,
Donna Stienstra, and Dean Miletich

Federal Judicial Center 1997

Reports on Discovery for the Advisory Committee on Civil Rules
of the Judicial Conference of the United States

This Federal Judicial Center publication was undertaken in furtherance of the Center's statutory mission to conduct and stimulate research and development for the improvement of judicial administration. The views expressed are those of the authors and not necessarily those of the Federal Judicial Center.

Contents

Foreword

Bench and bar have debated for at least thirty years how discovery in civil litigation operates and how it should operate and whether the Federal Rules of Civil Procedure regulate it too much or not enough. Center research has shed empirical light on this controversy at least since the District Court Studies Project, which was launched in 1973 at the instigation of Center Director Walter Hoffman. The reports in that series were of substantial assistance to the Judicial Conference rules committees. *Discovery and Disclosure Practice, Problems, and Proposals for Change* continues in that tradition.

The Center prepared this report at the request of the Advisory Committee on Civil Rules to provide an empirical context for the Committee's consideration of the need for change in the discovery rules. Based on responses from nearly 1,200 attorneys nationwide, the report provides a timely assessment of the effects of the 1993 amendments to the discovery rules, including initial disclosure. It also provides information about discovery costs in the context of the overall costs of civil litigation, about problems experienced by attorneys in a sample of recently terminated cases, and about attorneys' preferences for rule revisions and other changes that might improve discovery.

The authors presented the report to the Committee and other attendees at a Boston College symposium sponsored by the Committee on September 4–5, 1997. Additional analyses, included here as an addendum, were presented to the Committee at its October 6–7 meeting.

We are publishing this report because we hope and expect that it will stimulate and enlighten the evolving debate over the future direction of the discovery rules and at the same time preserve a record of the information provided to the Committee in September and October 1997 as the members begin their deliberations about possible discovery rule changes.

Rya W. Zobel
Director
Federal Judicial Center
November 1997

I. Background[1]

The Judicial Conference's Advisory Committee on Civil Rules requested that the Federal Judicial Center conduct research on questions relating to discovery. Judge Paul Niemeyer (4th Cir.), chair, appointed a subcommittee chaired by Judge David Levi (E.D. Cal.) to determine the questions to be studied and to work with the Center in designing the research. In response to the committee's request and in consultation with the subcommittee, the Center determined that a national survey of counsel in closed federal civil cases would address many of the committee's questions.

This report presents findings from a national survey of responses to a questionnaire mailed on May 1, 1997, to 2,000 attorneys in 1,000 closed civil cases. We sampled from cases in which discovery might be expected by excluding cases such as Social Security appeals, student loan collections, foreclosures, default judgments, and cases that were terminated within sixty days of filing. Questionnaires were returned by 1,178 attorneys, a response rate of 59%. The cases in which respondents were involved appear to be representative of the sample as a whole. For further information concerning the sample and its representativeness, see Appendix A. The questionnaire is attached at Appendix B.

The Committee's interests cover four broad areas of inquiry: (1) How much discovery is there and how much does it cost? (2) What kinds of problems occur in discovery and what is their cost? (3) What has been the effect of the 1993 amendments to the federal rules governing discovery? (4) Is there a need for further rule changes and if so what direction should they take? This report provides information in response to the following specific questions derived from these four general topics:

1. What kinds of discovery do attorneys use?

2. How much does discovery cost the parties? What are its costs relative to total litigation costs, to the amount at stake, and to the information needs of the case?

3. How often do problems arise in discovery? What kinds of problems arise? Do problems arise more often in particular types of cases?

4. What proportion of discovery expense is due to discovery problems?

5. With what frequency is initial disclosure used? What are its effects? What kinds of problems arise in initial disclosure?

6. With what frequency is expert disclosure used? What are its effects? What kinds of problems arise in expert disclosure?

7. With what frequency are the other 1993 discovery rule amendments used (meet-and-confer requirements, discovery planning, limits on deposition conduct, and limits on interrogatories and depositions)? What are their effects?

8. With what frequency does document production occur? What kind of problems arise in document production?

---

1. We acknowledge the valuable assistance of a number of Center staff members in various stages of producing this report, including Joe Cecil, George Cort, Melissa Day, Yvette Jeter, Pat Lombard, Naomi Medvin, Jackie Morson, Aletha Janifer, David Rauma, Elizabeth Wiggins, and Carol Witcher.

9. What are the expenses for specific discovery activities?

10. In the view of attorneys, what causes discovery problems? To what extent are discovery problems due to judicial case management?

11. Is nonuniformity in the disclosure rules a problem?

12. If change is necessary, what direction should it take? What changes would be most likely to reduce discovery expenses? Should change occur now or later?

II. Highlights from the Research

1. High levels of discovery problems and high expenses were more likely to occur in cases with high stakes, high levels of contentiousness, high levels of complexity, or high volumes of discovery activity. Problems in these cases were not limited to a particular procedural area, such as disclosure or document production, but occurred in most or all aspects of discovery.

2. Overall, 48% of attorneys who had some discovery in their case reported discovery problems. Document production generated the highest rate of reported problems.

3. Generally, discovery expenses represented 50% of litigation expenses and 3% of the amount at stake in the litigation.

4. Discovery expenses incurred unnecessarily because of problems averaged 9% of discovery expenses and about 4% of overall litigation expenses.

5. Depositions account for by far the greatest proportion of discovery expenses.

6. The total cost of litigation is most strongly associated with several other cost variables, especially the size of the monetary stakes. Total cost is also associated with the size of the law firm, the type of case, and whether the case was complex or contentious.

7. Initial disclosure is being widely used and is apparently working as intended, increasing fairness and reducing costs and delays far more often than decreasing fairness or increasing costs and delays. Attorneys reported that initial disclosure reduced litigation cost and time. Multivariate analyses confirmed these impressions for disposition time but not for litigation cost.

8. Independent of the rules, there was a considerable amount of informal exchange of discoverable information.

9. Expert disclosure generally appears to be working as intended by increasing procedural fairness. About a quarter of those who used expert disclosure said it had increased their litigation expenses, but, perhaps more surprisingly, 31% said it had decreased their expenses.

10. Increased judicial case management is the means attorneys most often recommended for alleviating discovery problems and reducing discovery expenses, but multivariate analyses failed to detect an association between judges' case management approaches and disposition times or litigation costs.

11. Disposition time is mostly strongly related to the monetary stakes, case complexity, percentage of costs due to depositions, and attorneys' reported use of hourly billing.

12. The nonuniformity of disclosure rules across districts presents only moderate problems for most attorneys. Nonetheless, the majority of attorneys want a uniform national rule.

13. Attorneys are split over the direction a uniform national rule should take. A large majority of those who have used initial disclosure favor a rule continuing initial disclosure. A large majority of those from districts that have opted out oppose a rule requiring initial disclosure.

III. Summary of the Research Findings

Set out below are the questions posed by the Advisory Committee on Civil Rules, along with short answers derived from the research. More detailed findings are reported in section IV. In most instances, the findings are reported by individual attorney responses, not by combining attorney responses for each case.

1. What kinds of discovery do attorneys use?

The Federal Rules of Civil Procedure have traditionally regulated the conduct of discovery according to the type of discovery activity used—e.g., depositions, document production, and interrogatories. For that reason, it is of interest to identify the kinds of activities that take place in the context of these rules and the problems that arise in using them.

In our sample, drawn from cases likely to have discovery, about 85% of the attorneys said some discovery activity had occurred in their case. This includes discovery planning, as well as formal discovery or disclosure. Of the 85% of cases that had some discovery activity, 94% of the attorneys reported that formal discovery occurred in their case (Tables 1 & 2).

The most frequent form of discovery activity was document production: 84% of those who said there was some discovery or disclosure in their case said they engaged in document production. Interrogatories and depositions also occurred at relatively high rates: 81% and 67% respectively. Fifty-eight percent (58%) of the attorneys reported that initial disclosure occurred in their case, and 29% said expert disclosure did (Table 2).

Nearly two-thirds of those who engaged in formal discovery or disclosure also informally exchanged discoverable information without being required by rule to do so (Table 1).

2. How much does discovery cost the parties? What are its costs relative to total litigation costs, to the amount at stake, and to the information needs of the case?

Of long-standing concern has been the cost of discovery and the relationship of that cost to the overall cost of litigation and the amount at stake in the case. Anecdotal information—

and the occasional horror story—suggests that discovery expenses are excessive and disproportionate to the informational needs of the parties and the stakes in the case.

Discovery expenses generally.

We found that the median cost of litigation reported by attorneys in our sample was about $13,000 per client (Table 3). About half of this cost was due to discovery (Table 4). The proportion of litigation costs spent on discovery differed little between plaintiffs and defendants. The factors most closely related to total litigation costs were the size of the monetary stakes, the size of the law firm, the type of case, and whether the case was complex or contentious (section VI).

Discovery relative to stakes.

Discovery expenses were quite low in relation to the amount at stake in the litigation. The median percentage was 3% of the stakes; however, a small percentage of the attorneys (5%) estimated discovery expenses at 32% or more of the amount at stake (Table 6). Total litigation costs were strongly associated with the monetary stakes in the case (section VI). About half the attorneys thought the expenses of discovery and disclosure were about right in relation to their client's stakes in the case. Fifteen percent (15%) thought the expenses were high and 20% said they were low relative to the stakes (Table 8).

Discovery relative to information needs.

Most attorneys—representing plaintiffs and defendants alike—thought the discovery or disclosure generated by the parties was about the right amount needed for a fair resolution of their cases. Fewer than 10% thought the process generated too little information, and about 10% thought the process generated too much information (Table 9).

3. How often do problems arise in discovery? What kinds of problems arise? Do problems arise in particular types of cases?

Over the past decade considerable concern has developed over what are perceived to be widespread problems with discovery. In our sample, 48% of the attorneys who used discovery or disclosure reported one or more problems. Of those who reported problems, 44% said problems occurred in document production, 37% said they occurred in initial disclosure, 27% in expert disclosure, and 26% in depositions (Table 10). When attorneys reported problems in one discovery activity, like depositions, they often reported problems in other discovery activities, particularly document production (Table 11).

Attorneys in tort and civil rights cases were more likely to report discovery problems than attorneys in contracts or other cases. Both the likelihood of problems and the total incidence of problems increased as stakes, factual complexity, and contentiousness increased.[2]

---

2. Throughout the report we will refer to "complex" and "contentious" cases, by which we mean cases rated by the attorneys as complex or contentious. We are reporting the attorneys' subjective assessments of

4.   What proportion of discovery expense is due to discovery problems?

About 40% of the attorneys reported unnecessary discovery expenses due to discovery problems. Where unnecessary expenses were reported, they amounted to about 19% of total discovery expenses (Table 12); overall about 4% of litigation expenses are attributable to discovery problems. A multivariate analysis did not suggest that the incidence of discovery problems was associated with litigation costs (section VI).

The *percentage* of unnecessary discovery expenses attributed to problems did not vary with the total amount of discovery expenses, suggesting that the higher incidence of problems and greater absolute cost in larger or more complex cases may simply be in proportion to the greater amount of discovery in such cases.

5.   With what frequency is initial disclosure used? What are its effects? What kinds of problems arise in initial disclosure?

The most controversial of the 1993 amendments is the revision of Fed. R. Civ. P. (hereafter Rule) 26(a)(1), which permits each district to determine whether to require attorneys to disclose specified types of information early in the litigation without requests from opposing counsel. The rule drafters intended to achieve a number of outcomes, including less formal discovery, lower litigation costs, and earlier settlements. Because Rule 26(a)(1) permits districts, as well as attorneys by stipulation, to opt out of the rule, it has been unclear how many cases have actually been subject to the rule, much less what its impact has been.

Frequency of initial disclosure.

We found that over half of the attorneys (58%) who engaged in some discovery or disclosure either provided or received initial disclosure in their case (Table 2). The vast majority of attorneys (89%) who reported that initial disclosure occurred in their case also reported other types of discovery, indicating that initial disclosure seldom replaces discovery entirely.

Given the unexpectedly high incidence of initial disclosure, we examined whether the cases in our sample might overrepresent the amount of disclosure. We concluded that they do not, but also found, surprisingly, that more than a third of the attorneys in our sample who had engaged in initial disclosure had litigated their case in a district classified as having opted out of Rule 26(a)(1)'s requirements (Table 15). These data, together with the finding that 58% of cases with some discovery also involved disclosure, suggest that initial disclosure requirements may be more prevalent than some believe.

Effects of initial disclosure.

In general, initial disclosure appears to be having its intended effects. Among those who believed there was an effect, the effects were most often of the type intended by the drafters of the 1993 amendments. Far more attorneys reported that initial disclosure

---

their cases, not an objective measure. In the interests of readability, however, we use the shorthand "complex case" and "contentious case."

decreased litigation expense, time from filing to disposition, the amount of discovery, and the number of discovery disputes than said it increased them. At the same time, many more attorneys said initial disclosure increased overall procedural fairness, the fairness of the case outcome, and the prospects of settlement than said it decreased them (Table 17).

Multivariate analysis using docket information about the time from filing to disposition supported attorneys' reports that initial disclosure is associated with a reduction in time from filing to disposition. Multivariate analysis, however, did not confirm attorneys' perceptions that initial disclosure was linked to a decrease in their clients' litigation costs (section VI).

Nonetheless, more than a third of the attorneys (37%) who participated in initial disclosure identified one or more problems with the process (and generally with other aspects of discovery in their cases). The most frequently identified problem was incomplete disclosure (19% of attorneys who participated in disclosure). Relatively few attorneys reported that disclosure requirements led to motions to compel, motions for sanctions, or other satellite litigation (Table 18). Problems in initial disclosure arose more frequently in cases involving large stakes and expenses or that were characterized as complex or contentious.

6. With what frequency is expert disclosure used? What are its effects? What kinds of problems arise in expert disclosure?

The 1993 revisions to Rule 26(a)(2) require attorneys, unless they stipulate otherwise, to provide opposing counsel a list of expert witnesses and, when appropriate, a written report summarizing the testimony to be offered by expert witnesses. Although it was likely that preparation of a written report might increase litigation costs, the rule drafters hoped it would enhance the amount of information available to each side and thus the fairness of the litigation.

Frequency of expert disclosure.

We found that most attorneys (73%) in our sample did not engage in expert disclosure. Of those who did, 71% said they provided an expert's written report to the opposing party (Table 19).

Effects of expert disclosure.

Like initial disclosure, expert disclosure appears to be having its intended effect, albeit with an increase in litigation expenses for 27% of the attorneys who used expert disclosure. That an expanded report may increase litigation expenses is not completely unexpected. Indeed, what may be more surprising is that slightly more attorneys—31%— reported decreased litigation expenses (Table 20).

Of the respondents who perceived an effect, far more said expert disclosure increased both overall procedural fairness and the fairness of the case outcome than said it decreased them. Many more also said expert disclosure increased pressure to settle than said it decreased such pressure (Table 20).

Of respondents in cases where expert disclosure took place, 27% reported problems with expert disclosure. The most frequent problems cited by attorneys were that expert disclosure was too brief or incomplete (13%), too expensive (9%), or not updated (9%) (Table 21).

7. **With what frequency are the other 1993 discovery rule amendments used (meet-and-confer requirements, discovery planning, limits on deposition conduct, and limits on interrogatories and depositions)? What are their effects?**

The 1993 rule revisions also brought several other changes. We discuss three—the requirement to meet and confer; the requirement to plan discovery; and the limits on the number of depositions and deposition conduct. Overall, multivariate analyses found no relationship between case-management activities and either litigation costs or the time from filing to disposition. The factors most closely related to disposition time were the monetary stakes in the case, the complexity of the case, the percentage of costs due to depositions, and attorneys' reports of billing on an hourly basis (section VI).

Meet and confer/discovery planning.

Amended Rule 26(f) requires parties to meet and confer to develop a proposed discovery plan prior to the court's scheduling conference, and amended Rule 16(b) in turn directs courts to "enter a scheduling order that limits the time . . . to complete discovery."

In our sample, about 60% of the attorneys reported that they met and conferred with opposing counsel. Most attorneys (72%) reported that a discovery plan was developed for their case. As was the case with the disclosure provisions, the majority of attorneys reported that meeting and conferring had no effect. The majority of those who reported effects said the effects were of the type intended by the rule drafters. That is, the process of meeting and conferring reduced overall litigation expenses, time from filing to disposition, and the number of issues in the case (Table 22). It was also seen as increasing overall procedural fairness and fairness of the case outcome.

Numerical limits on depositions.

The 1993 amendments revised Rule 30(a)(2)(A) to limit to ten the number of depositions that may be taken without court approval. For our sample of cases, 75% of attorneys who reported that depositions were used in their case said seven or fewer individuals were deposed, well within Rule 30's presumptive limit of ten depositions (Table 24). Only 4% of attorneys reported that too many depositions were conducted in their case (Table 25).

About 25% of the attorneys who had used depositions in the sample case (67% said they had) reported problems with this discovery tool. The most frequent complaint (12% of those who used depositions) was that too much time was spent on a deposition (Table 25). The median length of the longest deposition was four hours, and 25% of the longest depositions took seven hours or more (Table 24).

In 1991, the Advisory Committee considered but did not adopt a six-hour time limit on depositions. Had this limit been in effect, it appears it would have affected about 30% of the cases in our sample.

Deposition conduct.

In 1993, the Rules Committee also amended Rules 30(d)(1) and (3) to proscribe using objections in an argumentative or suggestive manner, to limit attorneys from instructing witnesses not to answer questions, and to provide consequences for other unreasonable conduct. In our sample, a small number of attorneys reported problems in three areas of deposition conduct: that an attorney coached a witness (10%), instructed a witness not to answer (8%), or otherwise acted unreasonably (9%) (Table 25). These responses suggest that the 1993 amendments have not entirely eliminated these problems.

8. With what frequency does document production occur? What kind of problems arise in document production?

Anecdote has suggested that document production is one of the most costly parts of discovery and is fraught with difficulties. As we will discuss shortly, it is not one of the most expensive forms of discovery. However, it is the discovery device most frequently used by attorneys (84%) and the activity for which the highest percentage of attorneys reported problems in their cases (44%).

The most frequently reported problems with document production were failure to respond adequately (28% of those who engaged in document production) and failure to respond in a timely fashion (24%) (Table 26). Those representing plaintiffs were more likely to complain that a party failed to respond adequately, while those representing defendants were more likely to complain that requests were vague or sought an excessive number of documents. Problems with document production are more likely to occur in high stakes, complex, or contentious cases, but a significant number of problems also occur in non-complex, non-contentious, and low-stakes cases.

9. What are the expenses for specific discovery activities?

Depositions accounted for by far the greatest amount of discovery expense (median = $3,500 in cases with depositions). The next most costly types of discovery were expert discovery and disclosure (median = $1,375), document production (median = $1,100), and interrogatories (median = $1,000). Less expense was incurred by initial disclosure (median = $750) and meeting and conferring/discovery planning (median = $600) (Table 28).

Document production, often said to be the most burdensome and costly part of discovery, typically involved rather modest costs. Nonetheless, devoting higher *percentages* of litigation cost to document production was related to higher total costs (section VI).

10. In the view of attorneys, what causes discovery problems? To what extent are discovery problems due to judicial case management?

Among four types of attorney/client conduct that might have contributed to discovery problems, attorneys were most likely to attribute problems to one or more attorneys' or parties' intentional delays and complications; 55% of the attorneys cited this as a cause of discovery problems. Smaller percentages attributed problems to lack of client cooperation, pursuit of disproportionate discovery, or incompetent or inexperienced counsel (Table 32).

When judges were involved in discovery, as they were for 81% of the attorneys in our sample, they were far more likely to have been involved in the planning phase of discovery than to have decided motions or imposed sanctions. The vast majority of attorneys (83%) found no problems with the court's management of disclosure or discovery. While no single problem area had a high level of reported problems (Table 33), the most frequent specific complaints were that the time allowed for discovery was too short (7%) and that the court was too rigid about deadlines (5%) (Table 33 and text).

11. Is nonuniformity in the disclosure rules a problem?

Although for some time there has been growing concern about nonuniformity in the Federal Rules of Civil Procedure, those concerns became greater after 1993 when the revisions to Rule 26 explicitly permitted districts to opt out of the rule's initial disclosure requirements. Since that time, an increasing number of voices among both the bench and bar have asserted that nonuniformity in the discovery rules—and in the disclosure rules in particular—is a serious problem and should be resolved.

That opinion is shared by the attorneys in our sample, at least with regard to nonuniformity of disclosure *across* districts. A clear majority—60%—of the attorneys with opinions on this subject said nonuniformity in the disclosure rules creates problems (Table 34). Most said the problems are moderate, but attorneys who practiced in four or more districts (10% of the respondents) are more likely than other attorneys to see such problems as serious. Even these national practitioners, however, are more likely to label the problems moderate than serious.

When asked about nonuniformity of disclosure requirements *within* districts, about 25% of the attorneys said there are problems with nonuniformity of disclosure rules within the district in which the sample case was filed. Almost half said there is no significant lack of uniformity within the district in which their case was filed (Table 34).

12. If change is necessary, what direction should it take? What changes would be most likely to reduce discovery expenses? Should change occur now or later?

Given the concerns that have been raised about problems in discovery, the costs of discovery, and the impact of nonuniformity, both judges and lawyers, as well as policymakers within and outside each group, have asked what should be done. Are additional rule changes needed, for example? Or should judges and attorneys modify their behavior in some way? We examined the question of change in several ways.

<u>What kind of reform holds the greatest promise for reducing discovery problems</u>?

In response to a list of thirteen changes that might potentially reduce litigation costs, the most frequent choice by the attorneys was to increase the availability of judges to resolve discovery disputes (54%). Adopting a uniform rule requiring initial disclosure ranked second (44%), followed by two changes that tied for third place: imposing sanctions more frequently and severely (42%) and adopting a civility code (42%) (Table 35).

When we combined these thirteen response options into a more limited set, judicial case management ranked first (63%), followed closely by changing attorney behavior through sanctions or civility codes (62%) (Table 36).

The attorneys were then asked which of three approaches—more judicial case management, further rule revisions, or attention to attorneys' and clients' economic incentives—holds the *most* promise for reducing problems in discovery. About half the attorneys said increased judicial case management holds the most promise. Only about a quarter called for revising the rules to further control or regulate discovery, while the other quarter called for addressing the need for changes in client/attorney incentives (Table 37).

<u>Do the discovery rules need to be changed? In what way should they be changed?</u>

Although attorneys view judicial case management as the most promising approach to reducing discovery problems, 83% nonetheless want changes in the discovery rules. The desire for change centers on initial disclosure.

Regarding initial disclosure, a plurality of all respondents in the sample—41%—favor a uniform national rule requiring initial disclosure in every district. Another 27% favor a national rule with no requirement of initial disclosure and with a prohibition on local requirements for initial disclosure. Close to a third—30%—favor the status quo. Attorneys who participated in initial disclosure in the sample case were considerably more likely to favor requiring disclosure than attorneys who did not (Table 39).

<u>When should changes be made</u>?

Among those who think the discovery rules should be revised, a majority (54%) favor making changes now (Table 42 and accompanying text). Most of that group consists of attorneys who want immediate consideration of change to Rule 26(a)(1).

IV. Detailed Results and Analysis[3]

1. What kinds of discovery do attorneys use?

<u>Frequency of discovery activities</u>.

Overall, about 85% of the attorneys in this national sample reported that some type of formal discovery activity—ranging from meeting and conferring to depositions and document production—occurred in their case.[4] For many of the 15% with no discovery, the case terminated relatively early: half in 180 days and 75% within a year of filing.

Table 1 shows the percentage of attorneys reporting each type of discovery activity when there was any discovery or disclosure in the case. The vast majority (94%) said some form of formal discovery—e.g., depositions, interrogatories, and so forth—had been conducted. Nearly three-quarters (72%) said a discovery plan or scheduling order had been entered in their case.

Table 1

Percentage of attorneys reporting that various general types of discovery and disclosure occurred, in cases involving some discovery or disclosure

Discovery activity	$(N = 886^*)$
Meeting and conferring re discovery plan (Q1)**	72%
Entry of discovery plan or scheduling order (Q3)	72
Informal exchange of discoverable information (Q4)	62
Initial disclosure (Rule 26(a)(1) or local provision) (Q5)	58
Either expert disclosure or expert discovery (Q9)	36
Expert disclosure (Rule 26(a)(2) or local provision) (Q9)	29
Formal discovery—Total (interrogatories, depositions, documents, requests for admissions, physical and mental examinations, subpoenas, inspections) (Q11 & Q12)	94

* Note that respondents could select more than one response. The percentages are based on the total number of responses in the subset of cases involving some discovery or disclosure and are not expected to equal 100%.

** "Q" refers to the question number in the questionnaire, which can be found at Appendix B.

---

3. Results are based on each attorney's responses about the case included in the sample. Plaintiff and defendant attorneys' responses from the same case have not been matched for these analyses. Using only those cases in which at least one plaintiff's and one defendant's attorney responded would diminish the number of useful responses to about 300 cases.

Appendix B contains a copy of the questionnaire. Most tables contain cross-references to the questions in the questionnaire.

Unless otherwise noted, we are relying on chi-square analyses when discussing differences between responses and are reporting only those differences that are statistically significant at the 0.05 level or better (i.e., the probability that the difference occurred by chance is at most 5%). Multivariate analyses are reported in an addendum (section VI).

4. Recall that the sample was drawn from cases likely to have some discovery (see Appendix A). The incidence of discovery in this study is thus likely higher than in studies that sample from all civil cases.

Table 2 presents a finer breakdown of the specific forms of discovery and disclosure reported by respondents. Document production is the most frequent form of discovery, reported by 84% of attorneys who used some discovery or disclosure in their cases, followed closely by interrogatories (81%). The next most common forms of discovery are depositions (67%) and initial disclosure (58%).[5] Other forms of discovery, including expert discovery, occur in fewer than a third of the cases.

Given that Rule 26(a)(1) had been in effect for about three years at the time we drew our case sample, and given that about half of the courts in the sample had opted out of the district-wide application of initial disclosure, the finding that 58% of attorneys reported initial disclosure activity may be somewhat surprising. As we will see below, a sizable portion of disclosure activity appears to result from use of initial disclosure by individual judges in districts that have formally opted out of the rule.

In subsequent sections, we will explore many of these forms of discovery in greater detail. We will not, however, give further attention to requests for admission or physical and mental examinations. Before leaving these discovery methods altogether, let us present two noteworthy items revealed by our data. First, requests for admission were more likely to be reported by attorneys in very contentious cases (54% of these attorneys) than by attorneys in cases rated as somewhat or not at all contentious (36%). Similarly, more attorneys in complex cases (40% of these attorneys) reported using requests for admission than did attorneys in cases that were somewhat complex (33%) or not at all complex (24%). Reported use of requests for admission was also more frequent when the stakes were greater than $150,000 (37% of these attorneys) than in lower stakes cases (25%).

Second, physical and mental examinations were more likely to be reported by attorneys in tort cases (26% of these attorneys), but a sizable number of attorneys in civil rights cases (9%) also reported that a medical examination was conducted. Not surprisingly, few attorneys in contracts cases (1%) and in a miscellaneous category of "other" civil cases[6] (3%) reported that medical examinations occurred in their cases.

---

5. Note that initial disclosure is a relatively recent addition to the discovery rules, with an effective date of December 1, 1993, though a few districts adopted a form of initial disclosure as part of their Civil Justice Reform Act Plan before the effective date of the federal rule. The sample includes cases to which the disclosure rules would not apply because the cases were filed before the effective date of the rule change or because they terminated prior to the time for filing disclosures (at or within ten days after the Rule 26(f) discovery planning meeting). Hence, the 58% of respondents reporting disclosure activity very likely understates the incidence of cases in which disclosure is now required.

6. "Other" cases are mostly federal statutory actions and labor cases. In the rest of the report, we will refer to these cases by the term "other."

Table 2
Percentage of attorneys reporting that specific forms of discovery and
disclosure occurred, in cases involving some discovery or disclosure*

Discovery activity	(*N* = 886)
Document production (Q12)**	84%
Interrogatories (Q12)	81
Depositions (Q11)	67
Initial disclosure (Rule 26(a)(1) or local provision) (Q9)	58
Requests for admission (Q12)	31
Expert disclosure (Rule 26(a)(2) or local provision) (Q9)	29
Expert discovery (Q9)	20
Physical or mental exam (Q12)	13
Other formal discovery (subpoenas, inspections) (Q12)	9

* Note that respondents could select more than one response. The percentages are based on the total number of responses in the subset of cases involving some discovery or disclosure and are not expected to equal 100%.

** "Q" refers to the question number in the questionnaire, which can be found at Appendix B.

<u>Informal exchange</u>.

While the findings discussed above are useful for understanding the extent to which attorneys use formal discovery, they also reveal that attorneys frequently engage in informal exchanges of information. Looking back at Table 1, we see that 62% of attorneys informally exchanged discovery information in cases where there was also some discovery or disclosure. In the cases in which attorneys reported no discovery or disclosure, 46% exchanged information informally.

Not surprisingly, informal exchanges were significantly more likely to occur in cases where relationships between the opposing sides were not contentious (64% of these attorneys informally exchanged information) than in very contentious cases (46%) or somewhat contentious cases (53%). What is surprising, though, is that informal exchanges occurred in about half of the contentious cases, suggesting this may be a well-established practice or that it is perhaps encouraged by some judges. Also, experienced attorneys were more likely than attorneys with less experience to report making voluntary exchanges; the rates increased from 50% of those with the least experience to 63% of those with the most experience. Such exchanges were more likely to be reported in tort cases (69%) than in contract (54%), civil rights (54%), or other cases (52%).

Attorneys who reported engaging in informal exchanges were less likely to report problems with discovery (38% reported problems) than were attorneys who did not engage in informal exchanges (58%). Similarly, attorneys who exchanged information informally were less likely to report problems with court management of discovery (15%) than were attorneys who did not exchange information informally (23%).

Though intriguing, these data do not tell us anything about cause and effect, only that there are differences between the group of attorneys who engage in informal exchange and those who do not. Are attorneys more likely, for example, to exchange information because they are not having problems with discovery, or are they less likely to have problems because they have informally exchanged information? Or there could be a causal relationship between these factors and an as yet unknown factor. We cannot tell, but the data suggest there may be a constellation of behaviors (and conditions, such as greater experience) that make for smoother discovery.

2.   **How much does discovery cost the parties? What are its costs relative to total litigation costs, to the amount at stake, and to the information needs of the case?**

Discovery expenses in general and relative to total litigation costs.

To understand the impact of discovery costs, it is important to examine them first in the context of overall litigation costs. We asked attorneys to estimate their total litigation expenses, including attorney fees, paralegal fees, and fees for such items as expert witnesses, transcripts, and litigation support services. For our sample of attorneys, the median total litigation costs per client were about $13,000 for cases involving any discovery expenses (Table 3).[7]

---

7. As with other data in this report, all figures pertaining to litigation expenses are reported on an attorney/client basis, not on a per case basis. Note also that we asked respondents to provide a dollar estimate for actual litigation expenses. We then asked for an estimate of the percentage of those expenses that were allocated to discovery and to particular types of discovery. We then applied these percentage estimates to the total dollar estimate to generate dollar estimates for discovery expenses.

Table 3
Total reported litigation expenses per client for cases involving
any discovery expenses[8] (Question 20*)

	All respondents (N = 899)	Plaintiffs (N = 415)	Defendants (N = 484)
95th percentile	$170,000	$200,000	$150,000
Median	13,000	10,000	15,000
10th percentile	2,300	2,000	3,000

* Refers to the question number in the questionnaire, which can be found at Appendix B.

Among attorneys reporting any discovery expense, the proportion of litigation expenses attributable to discovery is typically fairly close to 50%, as shown in Table 4. Half estimated that discovery accounted for 25% to 70% of litigation expenses. Both the mean and the median were about 50%, and there is no apparent difference between plaintiffs and defendants in this regard.

Table 4
Percentage of clients' total litigation expenses accounted for by discovery and disclosure, among
cases with some discovery expense (Question 21*)

	All respondents (N = 941)	Plaintiffs (N = 430)	Defendants (N = 511)
95th percentile	90%	90%	90%
Median	50	50	50
10th percentile	10	10	10
Mean	47	47	47

* Refers to the question number in the questionnaire, which can be found at Appendix B.

These data suggest that the typical case has rather modest litigation expenses—particularly relative to stakes, as we will see shortly—and that discovery expenses are a sizable but not surprising proportion of these expenses.

---

8. We report the 95th percentile, median, and 10th percentile for expenses and other monetary information to provide a reasonably thorough picture of the range of the results. The 95th percentile is the point on the distribution of responses that marks the divide between the top 5% of responses and the lower 95% of responses. In Table 3, in other words, 5% of respondents reported total expenses of $170,000 or more and 95% of respondents reported total expenses of $170,000 or less. Similarly, the 10th percentile marks the divide between the bottom 10% of responses and the upper 90% of responses. In Table 3, in other words, 10% of the respondents reported litigation expenses of $2,300 or less, and 90% reported expenses of $2,300 or more. The median—or midpoint—is, of course, the 50th percentile.

We do not report the mean litigation expense because it is inflated by extreme values above the 95th percentile and so does not reflect anything close to what is "normal" or "typical." This same observation applies to all means for discovery and litigation expenses expressed in monetary terms in this study.

Discovery expenses relative to stakes.

For purposes of understanding discovery and its contribution to litigation expenses, it is also important to examine discovery expenses relative to the stakes of the case. We estimated the monetary amount at stake in the case as the difference between respondents' answers to questions concerning the best and worst "likely outcomes" in the case. For this sample of cases, the median estimated monetary stakes per client were $150,000, with defendants estimating somewhat higher stakes than plaintiffs (Table 5).[9] Relative to these stakes, discovery expenses are very low—typically only 3% of the estimated stakes (Table 6). The proportion of discovery expenses relative to stakes is identical for plaintiffs and defendants.

Table 5
Estimated amount at stake per client (Question 23*)

	All respondents (*N* = 1,028)	Plaintiffs (*N* = 460)	Defendants (*N* = 568)
95th percentile	$5,000,000	$3,000,000	$5,500,000
Median	150,000	125,000	200,000
10th percentile	4,000	2,100	10,000

* Refers to the question number in the questionnaire, which can be found at Appendix B.

Discovery expenses typically amount to about 3% of the monetary stakes, whether the stakes are large or small. That is, when measured as a percentage of stakes, the amount spent on discovery is not correlated with stakes.[10] The *absolute dollars* spent on discovery are, however, correlated with the stakes. That is, as stakes rise the dollars spent on discovery also rise.

---

9. We measured the monetary amount at stake in the case as the difference between the best and worst "likely outcomes" reported by the attorneys. For example, if a plaintiff's attorney reported that the best likely outcome in a case was a $500,000 recovery and that the worst likely outcome was a $250,000 recovery, we calculated the stakes to be $250,000. Likewise, if a defendant's attorney reported the best likely recovery to be a $100,000 loss and the worst likely recovery to be a $500,000 loss, we calculated the stakes to be $400,000. We do not report the mean in Table 5 for the reasons cited in note 8, *supra*.

10. The Pearson correlation coefficient between the ratio of discovery expenses to stakes and the log of stakes is 0.10. The log is used because the Pearson coefficient assumes a linear relationship, and the log of stakes appears linearly related to discovery expenses as a percentage of stakes, while the absolute stakes are not linearly related to discovery expenses as a percentage of stakes.

Table 6
Discovery expenses as a percentage of amount at stake (Questions 21 & 23*)

	All respondents (N = 801)	Plaintiffs' attorneys (N = 361)	Defendants' attorneys (N = 440)
95th percentile	32%	32%	32%
Median	3	3	3
10th percentile	0.3	0.3	0.3

* Refers to the question number in the questionnaire, which can be found at Appendix B.

Monetary stakes may not be the only reflection of a case's importance to the parties. The case may, for example, involve a request for equitable relief not susceptible to monetary valuation, or a party may be concerned about the case's impact on future claims. Almost 25% of the attorneys reported that such nonmonetary issues were of dominant concern in their case (Table 7). Attorneys in civil rights cases (70% of them) and in "other" cases (64%) were especially likely to report that their clients had such concerns (compared to 43% of attorneys in contract cases and 34% in tort cases).

Table 7
Percentage of attorneys reporting the extent to which their client was concerned about nonmonetary relief or consequences beyond the monetary relief sought in the case (Question 24*)

Importance of nonmonetary consequences	All respondents (N = 1,022)	Plaintiffs' attorneys (N = 457)	Defendants' attorneys (N = 565)
Such consequences were of dominant concern**	23%	24%	21%
Such consequences were of some concern**	32	24	38
Such consequences were of little or no concern**	46	52	41

* Refers to the question number in the questionnaire, which can be found at Appendix B.

** The differences between plaintiffs' attorneys' and defendants' attorneys' responses are statistically significant.

Unlike the relationship we found between the amount of money spent on discovery and the amount at stake (i.e., as one rises the other does), we found no relationship between discovery expenses and nonmonetary stakes. That is, attorneys who reported that nonmonetary issues were of dominant concern to their clients were no more likely than other attorneys to have spent large sums of money on discovery. One possible explanation is that nonmonetary relief often arises in the context of a motion for a preliminary injunction. The truncated discovery schedule in such proceedings may serve to constrain discovery expenses.

We also examined the attorneys' subjective appraisals of the value of discovery in relation to stakes and found that 15% of attorneys thought discovery expenses were high relative to the stakes in their case, while 20% thought them to be low relative to stakes (Table 8).[11]

Table 8
Percentage of attorneys reporting whether discovery expenses, in
relation to stakes, were high, low, or about right (Question 30*)

	All respondents ($N = 1,089$)	Plaintiffs' attorneys** ($N = 497$)	Defendants' attorneys** ($N = 592$)
High	15%	17%	14%
About right	54	51	56
Low	20	20	20
No opinion	11	12	10

* Refers to the question number in the questionnaire, which can be found at Appendix B.

** The distribution of differences among plaintiffs' attorneys and defendants' attorneys is statistically significant.

An interesting question is whether sufficient information is obtained when discovery costs are low, especially when they are low relative to stakes. Some attorneys who had low costs relative to stakes, for example, may have found their information needs compromised. We found, to the contrary, that when attorneys reported that costs were low relative to stakes, by far the greatest proportion (88%) also reported that the information they obtained was about the right amount needed for a fair resolution of the case.[12] A mismatch between cost and usefulness of the discovered information was, in fact, more likely to occur when discovery costs were reported to be high relative to the stakes; 44% of attorneys who said costs were high relative to the stakes said the information obtained was more than the amount necessary for a fair resolution.

Discovery expenses relative to information needs.

In general, most attorneys (69%), including both plaintiffs' and defendants' attorneys, thought the discovery or disclosure generated was about the right amount needed for a fair resolution of the case (Table 9). Fewer than 10% thought the process generated too little information, and about 10% thought the process generated too much information. Plaintiffs' attorneys (12%) were considerably more likely than defendants' attorneys (5%) to report that discovery yielded too little information.

---

11. The mean percentage of discovery expenses unnecessarily incurred was about 15% for those who said the cost of discovery relative to stakes was low or about right (compared to about 30% for respondents reporting that discovery costs were high relative to the stakes).

12. Note that the analysis in this paragraph was done after removing the "No opinion" responses.

Table 9

Percentage of attorneys rating the amount of useful information discovered in relation to the informational needs of the case (Question 29*)

Amount of discovered information	All respondents (*N* = 1,094)	Plaintiffs' attorneys** (*N* = 499)	Defendants' attorneys** (*N* = 595)
Too much information	9%	6%	11%
About the right amount of information needed for a fair resolution	69	68	71
Too little information	8	12	5
No opinion	14	14	14

* Refers to the question number in the questionnaire, which can be found at Appendix B.

** The differences between plaintiffs' attorneys' and defendants' attorneys' responses are statistically significant.

3. **How often do problems arise in discovery? What kinds of problems arise? Do problems arise in particular types of cases?**

Frequency and nature of discovery problems.

Fifty-two percent (52%) of the attorneys in this sample reported that they had no problems with disclosure or discovery in their case. Defendants' attorneys (58%) were more likely than plaintiffs' attorneys (42%) to report that they had no problems. Of the attorneys who reported problems, 55% reported one to three types of problems, 22% reported four to five types of problems, and 23% reported more than five types of problems (responses are to a list of twenty potential problems relating to initial disclosure, document production, oral depositions, and expert disclosure).

Among the four types of discovery for which we examined the extent and nature of discovery problems, we found that document production generated the highest rate of problems (Table 10), with about half of the attorneys who had engaged in document production reporting one or more problems with the process. Thirty-seven percent (37%) of those who had engaged in initial disclosure encountered problems with this procedure, while depositions, which as we shall see consumed the most discovery dollars, caused the fewest problems.

Table 10

Percentage of attorneys reporting problems with document production, initial disclosure, expert disclosure, or depositions, in cases in which the activity occurred (Question 13*)

Discovery or disclosure procedure	Percentage
Document production ($N = 743$)	44%
Initial disclosure ($N = 517$)	37
Expert disclosure ($N = 259$)	27
Depositions ($N = 592$)	26

* Refers to the question number in the questionnaire, which can be found at Appendix B.

Table 11 shows the frequency with which discovery problems of one sort occur in tandem with problems of another sort. We see that when an attorney reported problems in one discovery activity, that attorney often reported problems in other discovery activities as well. Attorneys who identified problems with initial disclosure, for example, were also more likely to identify problems with document production—that is, 77% of those who said initial disclosure was a problem also said document production was a problem. These findings seem to suggest, as do those in the following section, that there may be problem cases rather than isolated problems with each separate form of discovery. These findings are consistent with a phenomenon we discussed earlier: that cases with larger amounts of discovery are more likely to have more discovery problems. Then, if cases with problems in disclosure, to take an example, include a disproportionate number of cases with large amounts of discovery, more of these cases will also have problems in other types of discovery.

Table 11

Percentage of attorneys reporting problems with document production, initial disclosure, expert disclosure, or depositions, by their reports for each other type of problem*

	Initial disclosure	Expert disclosure	Depositions	Document production
Initial disclosure ($N = 190$)	—	31%	41%	77%
Expert disclosure ($N = 69$)	68	—	51	81
Depositions ($N = 154$)	53	31	—	88
Document production ($N = 326$)	53	25	42	—
Problem rate for entire sample	37	27	26	44

* All of the differences in percentages of problems are statistically significant.

Discovery problems and nature of case.

In what turns out to be a common pattern, the presence of discovery problems differed by the type of case, size of monetary stakes in the litigation, complexity of the case, and contentiousness of relationships among attorneys and parties. Attorneys in tort cases (50% of attorneys in these cases) and civil rights cases (50%) were notably more likely to report discovery problems than were attorneys in contracts cases (36%) and "other" cases (43%). Discovery problems were also much more likely to be reported in cases with higher stakes. As the stakes increased from $4,000 or less (27% of these attorneys saying there were problems) to over $2 million (69%), the percentage reporting problems increased progressively. Likewise, 61% of attorneys in very complex cases reported problems with discovery, compared to 50% of attorneys in somewhat complex cases and 33% of attorneys in non-complex cases. On the contentiousness scale, 71% of attorneys in cases they rated as very contentious cases reported discovery problems, compared to 64% in somewhat contentious cases, and 29% in non-contentious cases.

Not only the presence but also the number of different types of discovery problems differed by monetary stakes, complexity, and contentiousness. Attorneys in cases valued over $150,000 (28% of these attorneys) were more than twice as likely to report multiple types of problems with discovery than attorneys in lower-stakes cases (12%). Likewise, attorneys in very complex cases (39% of them) were more likely to report multiple types of problems than were attorneys in somewhat complex cases (21%) and in non-complex cases (15%). And, attorneys in very contentious cases were more likely to report multiple types of problems (42%) than attorneys in somewhat contentious cases (22%) and in non-contentious cases (12%).

Again, the data suggest that problems in discovery may not differ so much by which form of discovery is used as they do by the nature of the case. Where a lot of money is at stake, where the issues involve personal injury or matters of principle, where the relationships are contentious and the issues complex, here we see more discovery and more problems with discovery.

We should not take these findings to suggest, however, that problems with discovery are more serious or more likely to occur as a *consequence* of case complexity, contentiousness, amount at stake, or amount of discovery expenses. Such cases have more discovery problems and more expenses associated with discovery problems than do other cases, but this may simply be due to their having greater amounts of discovery. A problem in conducting a deposition, for instance, may be as likely to occur if the deposition is in a small, non-complex case as it is if that deposition occurs in a large, complex case. The large case, however, may be more likely to have some deposition problems, but perhaps only because it has more depositions than the small case.

The increase in incidence and in types of problems associated with larger and more complex cases is consistent with the findings that discovery expenses bear about the same ratio to total expenses and amount at stake regardless of whether total expenses or stakes are large or small. We see a picture, then, where the stakes, expenses, and number of problems are proportional—as one increases, the others do, too.

4. What proportion of discovery expense is due to discovery problems?

About 40% of attorneys reported that some discovery expenses were incurred unnecessarily because of problems in discovery. The mean percentage of expenses due to discovery problems was 19% (Table 12).

Though the absolute cost of unnecessary discovery is greater in cases with higher stakes and higher overall costs, we found little correlation between the *percentage* of unnecessary discovery expenses and variables that might plausibly be related to those expenses, such as overall discovery expense, overall litigation expense, and amount at stake in the case.[13] In other words, the expenses due to *unnecessary* discovery appear to be proportional to the size of the case, just as we found for discovery expenses generally.

Table 12

Attorney estimates of the percentage of discovery expenses per client incurred unnecessarily because of problems in discovery (Question 14*)

	All respondents (N = 366)	Plaintiffs' attorneys (N = 168)	Defendants' attorneys (N = 198)
95th percentile	58%	75%	50%
Median	13	15	10
15th percentile[14]	2	2	2
Mean**	19	21	17

* Refers to the question number in the questionnaire, which can be found at Appendix B.

** The differences between plaintiffs' attorneys' and defendants' attorneys' responses are statistically significant.

The attorneys' estimates of expenses incurred unnecessarily because of discovery problems permit us to place a value on the financial significance of these problems. Using the percentage of attorneys who reported some problems with discovery (48%) and the mean percentage of discovery expenses attributed to such problems (19%) and applying those numbers to the entire sample, we estimate that about 9% (48% times 19%) of all discovery expenses are thought by attorneys to be incurred unnecessarily as a consequence of problems in discovery. Since discovery expenses account for about 47% of all litigation expenses, we estimate, further, that unnecessary discovery expenses represent about 4% (9% times 47%) of total litigation costs.

13. The Pearson correlation coefficients were 0.09 for amount at stake, 0.08 for discovery expenses, and 0.12 for litigation expenses.

14. We show the 15th rather than the 10th percentile here because the 10th percentile is 0%.

5. With what frequency is initial disclosure used? What are its effects? What kinds of problems arise in initial disclosure?

<u>Frequency and type of disclosure</u>.

Of the attorneys in cases with some discovery or disclosure, 58% said they provided or received initial disclosure in the sample case (Table 2). As noted earlier, this may be an underestimate of current practice, since some of the cases in the sample were filed before disclosure requirements were in effect or terminated before they reached the stage where disclosure would occur. As we will discuss below (Table 15 and text), a considerable amount of disclosure occurred in districts that had opted out of the Rule 26(a)(1) requirements.

The likelihood of having disclosure in a case does not vary systematically by readily identifiable characteristics of cases, such as case type or stakes. Disclosure occurred in contract, tort, civil rights, and "other" cases at approximately equal rates. Similarly, disclosure was no more or less likely to occur in low or high-stakes cases.

In the vast majority of cases in which attorneys reported that disclosure took place, they reported that discovery occurred as well (89%), indicating that disclosure infrequently replaces discovery entirely.

<u>Form of initial disclosure</u>.

For attorneys who engaged in initial disclosure under Rule 26 or local requirements, the most frequent form of disclosure included both lists and copies of documents (Table 13). About a quarter of those who engaged in disclosure, however, reported that their entire disclosure consisted of the documents themselves, even though Rule 26(a)(1) requires only a list or description of documents.[15] Altogether more than three-quarters of the attorneys reported that at least some copies were provided. More attorneys indicated that they disclosed documents and other information than indicated that they received such information.

Table 13
Percentage of attorneys reporting various forms of initial disclosure (Question 6*)

	All respondents (*N* = 499)	Plaintiffs' attorneys** (*N* = 215)	Defendants' attorneys** (*N* = 284)
Entire disclosure was in lists	23%	25%	22%
Entire disclosure was in copies of documents	28	29	27
Disclosure included lists and copies of documents	49	47	51

* Refers to the question number in the questionnaire, which can be found at Appendix B.

** None of the differences between plaintiffs' attorneys' and defendants' attorneys' responses are statistically significant.

---

15. Local rules in a few districts require that disclosure be in the form of copies, not lists, of documents.

Reasons for nondisclosure.

Of the 44% of attorneys who said there was no disclosure in their case, just about half reported that their case was exempt by district-wide local rules or other provisions (Table 14). Another 6% reported that their case was exempt by standing orders or because of case-by-case exemptions ordered by the district judge assigned to the case.

For the remaining half of the attorneys who had no disclosure it their case, it appears that disclosure rules were in effect in the district but were not applied in the sample case. This was usually for one of two reasons: (1) neither the parties nor the court took steps to initiate disclosure, or (2) disclosure did not apply because the case terminated before the disclosure deadline or was filed before disclosure rules went into effect. Very rarely did the parties stipulate out of disclosure.

Table 14
Percentage of attorneys reporting reason for lack of initial disclosure,
in cases in which there was no initial disclosure (Question 8*)

Reason	($N = 365$)
District exempted all cases or this type of case	49%
Assigned judge exempted all cases or this case	6
Parties stipulated that disclosure would not apply	4
No one began the process and court did not enforce disclosure	21
Rule 26(a) did not apply because case terminated early or case filed before the rule's effective date**	20

* Refers to the question number in the questionnaire, which can be found at Appendix B.

** These variables were added after recoding comments from "other" responses.

Prevalence of initial disclosure activity by district.

To determine whether the incidence of disclosure found in the study is unusually high, as some might suggest given the reported resistance to disclosure, we examined our sample in light of what we know about implementation of initial disclosure. Using available information about initial disclosure rules[16] to classify the practices of all the districts represented in the sample, we classified the districts as follows: (1) the national rule is fully in effect; (2) a less stringent form of initial disclosure is in effect by local rule or provision; (3) no disclosure is required by federal rule or local provision (opt-out); and (4) individual judges are authorized by local rule to require disclosure in individual cases.

We then examined the attorneys' responses to determine whether initial disclosure occurred in their case and matched those responses with the district in which the sample case was filed. What is noteworthy is that initial disclosure was reported in the sample

---

16. Donna Stienstra, Implementation of Disclosure in United States Courts (Federal Judicial Center 1997).

case by more than a third of the attorneys practicing in districts classified as having opted out of Rule 26(a)(1)'s requirements (Table 15). These data—and our finding above that 58% of cases with some discovery also involved disclosure—suggest that initial disclosure requirements may be more prevalent than some believe. Why disclosure occurred in cases in non-disclosure districts is not clear, but one possibility is that individual judges in these districts are requiring disclosure.[17]

Table 15

Percentage of attorneys who did and did not use initial disclosure in their case, by type of disclosure requirement in district in which the case was filed ($N = 1,178$)

	National rule in effect	Less stringent local variation	No disclosure required	Individual judge discretion
Disclosure	73%	73%	35%	37%
No disclosure	27	27	65	63

We also examined our sample population to determine whether the relatively high portion of cases subject to disclosure might be the result of a higher response rate from districts that require initial disclosure. By comparing the responses with the original sample, we were able to determine that this is not the case; the responses closely track the distribution of the sample cases (Table 16). The sample cases themselves are a random national sample, with no known characteristics that would make the sample unrepresentative of federal cases generally (with the proviso, of course, that the sample is drawn from cases likely to have discovery).

Table 16

Type of disclosure requirements in effect in the districts from which the sample cases were drawn and from which the responses were received*

	National rule in effect	Less stringent local variation	No disclosure required	Individual judge discretion
District of sample attorneys ($N = 2,015$)	31%	21%	26%	22%
District of responses ($N = 1,178$)	32	21	27	20

* None of the differences is statistically significant.

---

17. It is also possible that some attorneys misreported. Not likely, however, is that attorneys reported informal exchanges as disclosure, since the questions about each were quite precise in what they were seeking (Questions 4 & 5, Appendix B).

Perceptions of initial disclosure's effects.

When Rule 26 was amended in 1993, the rule drafters hoped it would have a number of effects, seven of which are shown in Table 17. For any single effect, at least a plurality, and usually a majority, of respondents did not see initial disclosure as having that effect. Altogether, however, more than 80% of the respondents said disclosure had at least one of the desired effects. Among those who reported an effect, the vast majority said the effect was in the direction intended by the drafters of the 1993 amendments.

Specifically, respondents who reported an effect were more likely to say that initial disclosure decreased their client's overall litigation expenses, the time from filing to disposition, the amount of discovery, and the number of discovery disputes. They also were more likely to say that initial disclosure increased overall procedural fairness, fairness of case outcome, and the prospects for settlement.

Table 17

Percentage of attorneys reporting specific effects of initial disclosure in their case (Question 7*)

Effect of initial disclosure on	Increased			Had no effect			Decreased		
	All	Pl.	Def.	All	Pl.	Def.	All	Pl.	Def.
Your client's overall litigation expenses ($N = 522$)	16%	16%	15%	45%	44%	46%	39%	40%	39%
Time from filing to disposition ($N = 508$)	7	9	5	62	57	65	32	33	31
Overall procedural fairness ($N = 508$)	37	39	36	54	50	57	9	11	7
Fairness of case outcome ($N = 500$)	25	26	24	70	67	72	5	6	4
Prospects of settlement ($N = 520$)**	36	38	34	59	53	63	6	9	3
Amount of discovery ($N = 522$)	10	13	8	47	46	47	43	41	44
Number of discovery disputes ($N = 483$)	5	7	4	62	57	66	33	36	30

* Refers to the question number in the questionnaire, which can be found at Appendix B.

** Differences between plaintiffs' attorneys' and defendants' attorneys' responses are statistically significant.

Attorneys' views of the efficacy of disclosure do not appear in general to differ by whether they represented plaintiffs or defendants. In only one instance—disclosure's effects on the prospects for settlement—do evaluations of disclosure's effects differ by party type, with plaintiffs' attorneys (38%) more likely than defendants' attorneys (34%) to see disclosure as increasing the prospects of settlement. Likewise, attorneys' evaluations of disclosure appear not to differ by the type of case being litigated or by the importance of nonmonetary issues.

At least one of disclosure's hoped-for benefits does, however, appear to differ by the size of the monetary stakes: attorneys in cases where monetary stakes were higher than $500,000 were less likely to report that initial disclosure increased overall procedural fairness (29% of these attorneys) than were attorneys in lower-stakes cases (40%). Moreover, in the higher stakes cases, plaintiffs' attorneys were notably more likely than defendants' attorneys to report a decrease in procedural fairness (25% vs. 7%). Along similar lines, as discussed in the next section, attorneys in cases with stakes over

$500,000 (43% of these attorneys) were more likely to find problems with initial disclosure, such as incompleteness, than were attorneys in lower-stakes cases (16%).

Reports of disclosure's efficacy also appear to differ by case complexity and contentiousness. Attorneys in complex cases (13% of these attorneys) were more likely than attorneys in non-complex cases (6% of these attorneys) to report that initial disclosure increased the amount of discovery conducted in their case. Similarly, attorneys in cases where relationships were contentious were more likely to say that initial disclosure increased the amount of discovery (27% vs. 8%) and increased litigation expenses (29% vs. 14%), while they were less likely to say disclosure increased the fairness of the outcome (19% vs. 26%).

In short, these responses suggest that there is a subset of cases—a combination of those with high stakes, high complexity, or contentious relationships—in which initial disclosure was not as effective as in other cases.

Problems with initial disclosure.

We saw earlier (Table 10) that 37% of the attorneys who participated in initial disclosure perceived one or more problems with its implementation. That rate of problem identification was somewhat higher than for depositions (26%) and expert disclosure (27%) but somewhat lower than for document production (44%).

As Table 18 shows, the incidence of any single type of problem with initial disclosure is modest. Complaints centered on incompleteness, failure to supplement, duplication, and lack of reciprocity. Satellite litigation was seldom mentioned.

Table 18

Percentage of attorneys reporting specific problems with initial disclosure, in cases where initial disclosure was reported (Question 13*)

Type of problem	All respondents (N = 517)	Plaintiffs' attorneys	Defendants' attorneys
Disclosure was too brief or incomplete	19%	21%	18%
A party failed to supplement or update the disclosures	12	12	13
Some disclosed materials were also requested in discovery	11	9	13
A party disclosed required information and another party did not disclose required information	11	12	10
Disclosure occurred only after a motion to compel or an order from the court	6	6	6
Other	3	2	3
Disclosure was excessive	2	3	2
Sanctions were imposed for failure to disclose	1	1	1

* Refers to the question number in the questionnaire, which can be found at Appendix B.

The incidence of reported initial disclosure problems differed meaningfully for several case characteristics. Problems were more likely to be reported in cases that lasted longer than a year, had monetary stakes greater than $500,000, were very complex, or involved very contentious relationships. On the other hand, we found no statistically significant differences between the presence of initial disclosure problems and the type of case, presence of nonmonetary stakes, type of party, practice setting, or number of years in the practice of law. Again, we see the difficulties in discovery—in this instance in initial disclosure—arising in cases that involve substantial sums of money and that are marked by complexity or contentiousness.

6. With what frequency is expert disclosure used? What are its effects? What kinds of problems arise in expert disclosure?

Frequency of expert disclosure and discovery.

Of the attorneys who had some discovery in their case, most (73%) did not report any expert discovery or disclosure. Of the 319 attorneys who did, 71% said they disclosed a written expert report to an opposing party pursuant to Rule 26(a)(2) or a similar local provision, and 57% reported receiving such a report (Table 19).

In cases that involved expert discovery or disclosure, about half of the attorneys reported participating in expert depositions. Only 4% of the attorneys who conducted expert discovery said they agreed not to disclose expert reports.

Table 19

Percentage of attorneys reporting that specific types of expert disclosure or discovery occurred in cases where some expert activity was reported (Question 9*)

Type of activity	(N = 319)
Provide written expert report under 26(a)(2) or local provision	71%
Receive written expert report under 26(a)(2) or local provision	57
Agree not to disclose expert report	4
Attend or conduct expert deposition	49
Conduct other expert discovery**	13

* Refers to the question number in the questionnaire, which can be found at Appendix B.

** Respondents reported, among other things, that they designated experts, sent or received expert interrogatories, or examined expert evidence such as medical records.

Attorneys in tort cases (46% of these attorneys) were far more likely to have engaged in expert disclosure than were attorneys in contracts (13%), civil rights (17%), or "other" (13%) cases. Attorneys who rated their cases as very or somewhat complex and whose cases lasted longer than a year were also more likely to report that expert disclosure occurred in their case. As the monetary stakes increased, the likelihood of expert disclosure increased progressively from 10% of attorneys in cases with less than $4,000 at stake to 36% of attorneys in cases with more than $2 million at stake. The likelihood of engaging in expert disclosure did not differ, however, by the importance of nonmonetary stakes.

<u>Perceptions of the effects of expert disclosure</u>.

The most frequent response to questions about expert disclosure's effects was that it had none (Table 20). Attorneys were especially unlikely to see an effect on disposition time, settlement pressures, and fairness of the case outcome. At most, just under half the attorneys reported that one of the benefits of expert disclosure—increased procedural fairness—had been achieved. If, however, we consider responses to all five possible effects, over two-thirds of the attorneys reported that at least one of the intended benefits was realized in their case.

Regarding litigation expenses, 27% of the attorneys who had engaged in expert disclosure reported that it increased expenses, a not-unexpected outcome given the requirement for a more comprehensive expert's report. When asked separately, however, about the expense of expert disclosure, only 9% reported that it was too expensive, suggesting that perhaps some of the added cost was expected and is not seen as problematic.

More surprising in some ways is the 31% who said expert disclosure decreased litigation expenses. Perhaps for some of these attorneys the written report served as a substitute for an expensive deposition, as the drafters of Rule 26(a)(2) hoped.

Table 20
Percentage of attorneys reporting specific effects of expert disclosure,
in cases where expert disclosure was reported (Question 10*)

Effect of expert disclosure requirement on	Increased			Had no effect			Decreased		
	All	Pl.	Def.	All	Pl.	Def.	All	Pl.	Def.
Client's overall litigation expenses (N = 241)	27%	31%	22%	43%	40%	46%	31%	29%	32%
Time from filing to disposition (N = 232)	10	14	7	72	69	75	18	17	19
Overall procedural fairness (N = 234)**	47	49	45	46	40	51	8	12	4
Fairness of case outcome (N = 231)	37	38	37	56	52	60	7	10	3
Pressure to settle (N = 230)	37	41	32	61	55	66	3	3	3

* Refers to the question number in the questionnaire, which can be found at Appendix B.

** Differences between plaintiffs' attorneys' and defendants' attorneys' responses are statistically significant.

Whether or not expert disclosure increased or decreased litigation expenses, attorneys often perceived it as increasing procedural fairness, although those who said it decreased litigation expenses were far more likely to say it increased procedural fairness (68%) than were those who said it increased litigation expenses (40%). Both groups, however, reported increased procedural fairness far more often than they reported decreased fairness, suggesting that even when expert disclosure increases expenses it is often seen as increasing procedural fairness as well.

Problems with expert disclosure.

Among the four principal types of discovery examined earlier (Table 10), expert disclosure had the second lowest rate of reported problems—27% of the attorneys who used expert disclosure encountered problems with it. When we look more closely at the specific kinds of problems that arose in expert disclosure, we find that the most frequent problem referred to disclosures that were too brief or incomplete, reported by 13% of the attorneys (Table 21). Others reported that the process was too expensive (9%) or that a party failed to supplement or update its expert disclosures (9%).

Table 21

Percentage of attorneys reporting problems with expert disclosure in cases where expert disclosure was reported (Question 13*)

Type of problem	All respondents (*N* = 259)	Plaintiffs' attorneys** (*N* = 124)	Defendants' attorneys** (*N* = 135)
Expert disclosure was too brief or incomplete	13%	11%	14%
Expert disclosure was too expensive	9	10	8
A party failed to supplement or update its disclosures	9	6	12
Other	4	3	5

* Refers to the question number in the questionnaire, which can be found at Appendix B.

** Differences between plaintiffs' attorneys' and defendants' attorneys' responses are not statistically significant.

Attorneys in cases with stakes higher than $500,000 were twice as likely to report problems with expert disclosure as attorneys in lower-stakes cases (about 40% vs. 20%). Likewise, attorneys in very contentious cases (54% of them) and somewhat contentious cases (32%) were far more likely to report expert disclosure problems than attorneys in non-contentious cases (15%).

Overall, however, the incidence of problems is quite low and notably lower than the number of attorneys who encountered problems with initial disclosure (37%) and document production (44%).

7. **With what frequency are the other 1993 discovery rule amendments used (meet-and-confer requirements, discovery planning, limits on deposition conduct, and limits on interrogatories and depositions)? What are their effects?**

A. Meeting and conferring

Discovery planning.

About 60% of the attorneys reported that they met and conferred with opposing counsel, either by telephone, correspondence, or in person, to plan for discovery in accordance with Rule 26(f) or a similar local provision.

Attorneys in complex cases (69% of these attorneys) were more likely to have met and conferred than attorneys in cases that were not complex (54%), but even the majority of those in non-complex cases had such conferences. The frequency of meeting and conferring did not differ meaningfully by type of case, size of monetary stakes, the presence of nonmonetary stakes, or the contentiousness of the parties. Further, the likelihood of meeting and conferring appears not to be related to the number of discovery problems or case-management problems reported by the attorneys.

One purpose of meeting and conferring is to develop a plan for discovery: other methods for developing a discovery plan are also available, and therefore to determine the number of attorneys whose cases were subject to discovery planning, we included those who had met and conferred, those who reported that the court issued a discovery plan or scheduling order, or both. We found that for the great majority of attorneys in our sample—77%—a discovery plan or scheduling order had been entered in their case. A plan or order was especially likely in cases where the attorneys had met and conferred—64% of these attorneys reported a plan or order—but even for about half of the attorneys who did not meet and confer, a plan or order was entered (Table 22).

Table 22

Percentage of attorneys reporting that they met and conferred, by percentage of reported issuance of discovery plan or scheduling order (Question 1 by Question 3*)

	Discovery plan or scheduling order	No discovery plan or scheduling order	Total
Meet and confer	64%	11%	75%
No meet and confer	13	12	25
Total (*N* = 1,035)	77	23	100

* Refers to the question number in the questionnaire, which can be found at Appendix B.

Not surprisingly, discovery planning and orders were less likely to be entered in cases with no formal discovery or disclosure. Along similar lines, cases terminated within 180 days were less likely to have discovery plans or scheduling orders. The incidence of discovery planning differed little by other case characteristics, such as the size of the monetary stakes, complexity, contentiousness, or nature of suit.

Among the attorneys who reported that a scheduling order or discovery plan had been issued, 90% also reported that the judge had held a conference to consider a discovery plan. For only 10% of the attorneys, then, was the scheduling order or discovery plan entered without consultation with the judge.

The median time limit imposed for completion of discovery was six months, with 75% of the attorneys reporting that they were limited to eight months or less. Although complaints about judicial management of discovery were uncommon, the two most frequently cited problems were that the time allowed for discovery was too short (7% of all respondents) and that the court was too rigid about deadlines (5%).

Perceived effects of meeting and conferring/discovery planning.

The majority of the 60% of attorneys who had met and conferred did not think meeting and conferring had any effect on litigation expenses, disposition time, fairness, or the number of issues in the case (Table 23). For those who thought there had been an effect, however, the effect was most often in the desired direction: lower litigation expenses (29%), shortened disposition time (29%), greater procedural fairness (33%), greater outcome fairness (21%), and fewer issues in the case (24%).

Table 23
Percentage of attorneys reporting specific effects of meeting and conferring* (Question 2**)

Effect of meeting and conferring on	Increased			Had no effect			Decreased		
	All	Pl.	Def.	All	Pl.	Def.	All	Pl.	Def.
Client's overall litigation expenses ($N = 646$)	17%	17%	18%	54%	56%	51%	29%	27%	31%
Time from filing to disposition ($N = 623$)	9	11	8	62	58	65	29	31	28
Overall procedural fairness ($N = 619$)	33	33	33	61	59	62	7	8	5
Fairness of case outcome ($N = 597$)	21	20	22	73	73	73	5	7	4
Number of issues ($N = 619$)	6	7	6	70	71	68	24	22	26

 * None of the differences between plaintiffs' attorneys' and defendants' attorneys' responses are statistically significant.

** Refers to the question number in the questionnaire, which can be found at Appendix B.

B. Depositions

Frequency of depositions.

For attorneys whose cases involved some discovery or disclosure, 67% reported that depositions had been conducted in their case (Table 2). The median number of *individuals* deposed was four and the mean was six (Table 24). Twenty-five percent (25%) of the attorneys reported that only one or two individuals were deposed, and for 75% of the attorneys no more than seven individuals were deposed.

The median number of *hours* spent by these attorneys in all depositions was ten. Again, the lowest 25% spent no more than five hours in depositions, while 75% of the attorneys spent no more than twenty-four hours in depositions. The high mean number of hours—twenty-five compared to a median of ten—suggests there were a small number of cases with a very high number of hours. Overall, however, the median length of the longest deposition is only four hours, and 75% of the attorneys reported that the longest deposition was no longer than seven hours.

In 1991, the Advisory Committee on Civil Rules proposed but did not adopt a six-hour limit on the length of depositions. Had a six-hour limit been in effect it would have affected about 30% of the cases; in those cases the district judge would have been authorized to make exceptions on a case-by-case basis.

Table 24
Frequency and length (hours) of reported depositions (Question 11*)

	Number of deponents (N = 592)	Average length (N = 579)	Total hours (N = 587)	Length of longest deposition (N = 572)
75th percentile	7	5	24	7
Median	4	3	10	4
25th percentile	2	2	5	3
Mean	6	4	25	6

* Refers to the question number in the questionnaire, which can be found at Appendix B.

Attorneys were more likely to have participated in depositions in tort cases (83% of these attorneys) and civil rights cases (81%) than in contract cases (58%) or "other" cases (57%). The likelihood of depositions also differed by the stakes in the litigation and the complexity of the case but not the contentiousness of the case. Among attorneys in cases with more than $2 million at stake, 85% had participated in depositions, while 50% of those with less than $4,000 at stake had depositions. Likewise, among attorneys in very complex cases, 81% had participated in at least one deposition, compared to 72% of attorneys in somewhat complex cases and 67% in non-complex cases.

Problems with depositions.

Far fewer attorneys reported problems with deposition practice (26% of those who reported any discovery problems) than reported problems with document production (44%), the most problematic form of discovery. The most frequent specific complaints about depositions were that too much time was taken (12% of those who participated in a deposition) or that an attorney coached a witness during a deposition (10%) (Table 25).

In 1993, the Rules Committee also amended Rules 30(d)(1) and (3) to proscribe using objections in an argumentative or suggestive manner, to limit attorneys from instructing clients not to answer questions, and to provide consequences for other unreasonable conduct. In our sample, small numbers of attorneys reported problems in three areas of deposition conduct: that an attorney coached a witness (10%), instructed a witness not to answer (8%), or otherwise acted unreasonably (9%) (Table 25). These responses suggest that the 1993 amendments have not entirely eliminated these problems.

This study was not designed, however, to identify the incidence of such behavior before 1993 and thus cannot test what the incidence would have been if the amendments had not been adopted.

Few respondents (4%, or twenty-five attorneys) reported that there were too many depositions. Of those who did, 75% reported participating in eight or more depositions, and 50% reported participating in fifteen or more depositions. Moreover, half of these attorneys reported spending more than fifty hours in depositions, and 25% reported spending 120 or more hours in depositions.

Table 25

**Percentage of attorneys reporting problems with depositions,
in cases where there were depositions (Question 13*)**

Type of problem	All respondents ($N = 579$)	Plaintiffs' attorneys** ($N = 257$)	Defendants' attorneys** ($N = 322$)
Too much time was taken in some or all depositions	12%	14%	11%
An attorney coached a witness during a deposition	10	10	11
An attorney acted unreasonably to annoy, embarrass, or oppress the deponent or counsel	9	11	7
An attorney improperly instructed a witness not to answer	8	9	7
There were too many depositions	4	4	5
Other	3	3	3

* Refers to the question number in the questionnaire, which can be found at Appendix B.

** None of the differences between plaintiffs' attorneys' and defendants' attorneys' responses are statistically significant.

Plaintiffs' and defendants' attorneys did not differ in their reports of problems with depositions, whether considering number, length, or attorney conduct. Problems were reported far more frequently, however, in complex cases, contentious cases, and civil rights cases. Among attorneys in very contentious cases, 66% reported problems, while 35% of those in somewhat contentious cases and 10% in non-contentious cases did. Among attorneys in civil rights cases, 35% reported deposition problems, compared to 22% of attorneys in tort cases and 13% in contract cases. Finally, attorneys in very complex cases were far more likely to report deposition problems (41% of them) than were attorneys in somewhat complex (24%) or non-complex (22%) cases.

8. With what frequency does document production occur? What kinds of problems arose in document production?

A request for production of documents was the discovery device most frequently used by attorneys in our sample, reported by 84% of those who said some discovery or disclosure activity had taken place in their case (Table 2). Document production also generated the highest rate of reported problems; 44% of the attorneys who said document production occurred in their case reported one or more types of problems with this discovery activity (Table 10).

The most common problems in document production were failure to respond adequately (28% of attorneys who engaged in document production) and failure to respond in a timely fashion (24%) (Table 26). Those representing plaintiffs were more likely to complain that a party failed to respond adequately (33% v. 24%), while those representing defendants were more likely to complain that requests were vague (20% v. 12%) or sought an excessive number of documents (19% v. 11%).

Table 26

Percentage of attorneys reporting problems with document production,

in cases where document production was reported (Question 13*)

Type of problem	All respondents ($N = 743$)	Plaintiffs' attorneys ($N = 335$)	Defendants' attorneys ($N = 408$)
A party failed to respond adequately**	28%	33%	24%
A party failed to respond in a timely fashion	24	25	24
One or more requests were vague**	16	12	20
An excessive number of documents were requested**	15	11	19
Materials provided were excessive or disordered	8	10	7
Other	3	4	2

* Refers to the question number in the questionnaire, which can be found at Appendix B.

** Differences between plaintiffs' attorneys' and defendants' attorneys' responses are statistically significant.

Document production problems were far more likely to be reported by attorneys whose cases involved high stakes, but even in low-to-medium stakes cases ($4,000 to $500,000), 36% of the attorneys reported problems with document production. In cases involving $500,000 to $2 million, 56% of attorneys reported such problems, and in cases involving more than $2 million, 75% reported document production problems.

In a similar vein, attorneys were far more likely to report document production problems in cases they labeled as very complex (66% of these attorneys) than in cases that were somewhat complex (44%) or not at all complex (35%). And attorneys were more likely to report such problems in very contentious cases (77% of these attorneys) than in somewhat contentious cases (54%) or in cases that were not at all contentious (29%).

Of all the discovery devices we examined, document production stands out as the most problem-laden. While the causes are elusive, the characteristics of complexity and contentiousness more often mark the cases where attorneys report document production problems. Despite these problems, however, document production is not the most costly part of discovery, as we shall see in the next section.

9.   What are the expenses for specific discovery activities?

Earlier we reported on the overall expense of discovery (section IV.2) and the proportion of discovery expenses attributable to discovery problems (section IV.4). In this section, we report the costs of several specific discovery activities.

Table 27 shows the mean percentage of discovery expenses allocable to each of the principal types of discovery. That is, considering the total costs of discovery, what portion of it is due to each of the seven activities listed in the table?

We see that, for our sample of attorneys, depositions accounted for almost one-third of all discovery expenses, while production of documents (16%), initial disclosure (16%), and interrogatories (13%) accounted for substantially less, and expert disclosure consumed only a small portion of all discovery expenses. For each discovery activity, there was no meaningful difference between the percentages reported by plaintiffs' and defendants' attorneys.

Table 27
Allocation of discovery expenses for cases with some discovery expense*
(Questions 20, 21, & 22) ($N = 921$)**

| | Mean percentage of discovery expenses | | |
Discovery activity	All	Plaintiffs' attorneys	Defendants' attorneys
Depositions	30%	29%	31%
Initial disclosure	16	17	16
Request for and/or production of documents	16	15	16
Interrogatories	13	13	13
Meet and confer/discovery planning	12	12	13
Expert disclosure or discovery	6	8	5
Other discovery activities	6	6	6

* None of the differences between plaintiffs' attorneys' and defendants' attorneys' responses are statistically significant.

** Refers to the question number in the questionnaire, which can be found at Appendix B.

The fact that expert discovery accounts for only 6% of all discovery expenses does not, however, imply that expert discovery is a low-cost activity. Table 27 is based on all cases in which there was some discovery, a large number of which had no expert discovery or disclosure. Thus, the percentage of discovery costs attributable to expert discovery is probably due to the relatively low number of cases with any such expense.

To correct for this problem, Table 28 provides information about the typical cost of each type of activity when that activity occurred in the case. It shows that when expert discovery occurred, it was the second most expensive of the discovery activities, with median expenses of $1,375 per client. The most expensive discovery activity, by a considerable margin, was depositions, with median costs per client of $3,500.

At least two notable points emerge from Tables 27 and 28. First, depositions accounted for about twice as much expense as any other discovery activity, whether on the basis of overall discovery expense (Table 27) or on the basis of deposition expense among cases with any deposition expense (Table 28). Second, production of documents did not result in unusually high expenses. Even at the 95th percentile (i.e., only 5% of attorneys reported higher costs than this), the expenses for document production were lower than expenses for depositions and expert disclosure.

Table 28
Expenses per client for indicated discovery activity, for cases with some such activity
(Questions 20, 21, & 22*)

Activity	95th percentile	Median	10th percentile
Depositions ($N = 602$)	$56,000	$3,500	$440
Expert disclosure or discovery ($N = 342$)	31,000	1,375	160
Other ($N = 179$)	21,000	1,300	110
Request for and/or production of documents ($N = 682$)	23,000	1,100	150
Interrogatories ($N = 658$)	16,000	1,000	160
Initial disclosure of documents ($N = 608$)	9,000	750	105
Meet and confer/discovery planning ($N = 672$)	8,800	600	75

* Refers to the question number in the questionnaire, which can be found at Appendix B.

Because we expected document production to represent very large expenses in at least a notable minority of cases, we pursued separate analyses of total discovery expenses and of document production expense for different types of cases. Tables 29 and 30 show the results. Both tables suggest that cases with very high overall discovery expenses and very high expenses for document production tend to arise in the miscellaneous category of "other" cases rather than in contract, tort, or civil rights cases.

Table 29

Discovery expenses per client by type of case, for cases with some discovery expense
(Questions 20 & 21*)

Case type	95th percentile	Median	10th percentile
Tort ($N = 236$)	$88,000	$6,600	$750
Civil rights ($N = 240$)	58,000	5,700	490
Contract ($N = 199$)	64,000	4,000	300
Other ($N = 224$)	300,000	4,000	400

* Refers to the question number in the questionnaire, which can be found at Appendix B.

Table 30

Expenses per client for requests for document production, for cases with such expense[18]
(Questions 20, 21, & 22*)

Case type	95th percentile	Median	10th percentile
Contract ($N = 151$)	$15,600	$975	$150
Tort ($N = 190$)	17,600	1,100	150
Civil rights ($N = 182$)	10,800	1,200	120
Other ($N = 159$)	88,200	1,250	165

* Refers to the question number in the questionnaire, which can be found at Appendix B.

Examining the "other" category more closely revealed that patent, trademark, securities, and antitrust cases stood out for their high discovery expenses. Table 31 shows the breakdown of discovery expenses for all patent, trademark, securities, and antitrust cases in our sample, along with the same information for all other types of cases and for those other cases involving at least $40,000 in discovery expenses. This permits comparison of two groups of high-expense cases and all other cases. It also allows us to see whether particular types of discovery are responsible for high discovery expenses.

---

18. Plaintiff and defendant expenses associated with document production differed only modestly. Both the median and 80th percentiles were about 50% higher for plaintiffs in contract cases, but higher for defendants in all other case types (about 40% higher in civil rights cases, 25% higher in tort cases, and 10% higher in other cases).

Table 31
80th Percentile of discovery expenses by type of discovery activity,
for respondents reporting any discovery expense[19]

Activity	80th percentile, patent, trademark, securities, and antitrust cases (N = 53)	80th percentile, all other cases with at least $40,000 discovery expenses (N = 105)	80th percentile, all other cases (N = 888)
Meet and confer/discovery planning	$12,000	$10,000	$1,250
Initial disclosure of documents	2,400	12,000	1,600
Expert disclosure or discovery	42,000	11,000	1,100
Depositions	135,000	51,000	7,400
Request for and/or production of documents	67,000	27,000	2,900
Interrogatories	47,000	18,000	2,300

Table 31 suggests that no particular type of discovery is the culprit responsible for excessive discovery expenses. We singled out patent, trademark, securities, and antitrust cases as a group because that group generally has high discovery expenses, but the distribution of those expenses across types of discovery activity does not differ notably from the distribution in other cases. Deposition expenses are very high, but not disproportionately so, compared to either cases with expenses of at least $40,000 or all other cases.[20]

10. In the view of attorneys, what causes discovery problems? To what extent are discovery problems due to judicial case management?

Attorney/client causes of discovery problems.

To what extent do attorneys and clients contribute to problems with discovery? About one-half to two-thirds of the attorneys in our sample did not think any of the four attorney/client causes we listed was a contributing factor to discovery problems, as shown in Table 32. More than half of the attorneys, however, identified intentional delays or complications as a moderate or major cause of discovery problems, and about 40% said lack of client cooperation, pursuit of disproportionate discovery, and incompetence or inexperience of counsel contributed to discovery problems.

---

19. We report the 80th percentile here because not all respondents reported expenses in every category, so lower percentiles reflect values too small to be informative. Because of the extreme expenses reported in a few instances, the mean is similarly uninformative.

20. Although it appears that the expenses for some discovery activities increase significantly more than for others, the differences are not likely to be statistically significant due to the limited number of responses and the fact that we focus here on the 80th percentile.

Table 32

Percentage of attorneys reporting the contributions made by attorneys and clients to problems with discovery, in cases with perceived discovery problems (Question 15*)

Contributing factor/ level of contribution	None			Moderate			Major		
	All	Pl.	Def.	All	Pl.	Def.	All	Pl.	Def.
Intentional delays or complications (*N* = 332)**	45%	38%	53%	28%	28%	28%	27%	35%	19%
Lack of cooperation by a client (*N* = 325)	54	52	57	29	27	30	17	21	14
Pursuit of discovery disproportionate to the needs of the case (*N* = 348)	62	66	59	21	20	22	17	14	19
Incompetence or inexperience of counsel (*N* = 337)**	59	73	48	22	15	27	19	12	25

* Refers to the question number in the questionnaire, which can be found at Appendix B.

** Differences between plaintiffs' attorneys' and defendants' attorneys' responses are statistically significant.

Plaintiffs' attorneys were considerably more likely to attribute perceived discovery problems to intentional actions by a party or attorney (63% v. 47%). Defendants' attorneys, on the other hand, were more likely to attribute problems to the incompetence or inexperience of counsel (52% v. 27%). On the whole, these data suggest that intentional activity is thought to play a significant role in creating discovery problems.

Judicial causes of discovery problems.

When judges were involved in discovery, as 81% of the attorneys said they were, they were far more likely to have been involved in the planning phase of discovery than to have decided motions or imposed sanctions. Of the instances in which attorneys reported some court involvement in discovery or disclosure, the court imposed time limits on the completion of discovery in 80% of those instances. The median time limit imposed by the court was six months; 75% of the limits were shorter than eight months, and 25% were four months or less.

Of the instances in which a judge was reported to have been involved in discovery or disclosure, 57% of attorneys indicated the judge held a conference—by telephone, correspondence, or in person—to consider a discovery plan; 42% reported that the judge discussed discovery issues at another conference; 25% said the court ruled on a discovery motion; and 20% said the court enforced the federal rules' limits on the number of interrogatories and depositions.

Presented with a list of nineteen types of potential court-management problems and an invitation to report any other problems, the vast majority of attorneys (83% of those in cases with some discovery or disclosure) reported no problems with the court's management of disclosure or discovery. Most of the specific problems were encountered by 2% or fewer of the attorneys who had some discovery in their cases. The problems most often encountered by attorneys—which were encountered by few—were the following: the time allowed for discovery was too short (7% of those in cases with some discovery), the court was too rigid about deadlines (5%), and rulings on discovery motions took too long (4%).

Overall, the problems with court management of discovery can be collapsed into four groups, as in Table 33. While the findings do not suggest a high level of court-management problems, it appears that the most frequent problem area is planning and implementation. Within that activity, the most frequent complaints were that the time allowed for discovery was too short (8%) and that courts were too rigid about deadlines (5%). Regarding discovery limits, few attorneys complained that limits on time or on the amount of discovery were too loose or that judges were too willing to grant extensions. In fact, they were as likely to say limitations were too restrictive as to say they were too lenient.

Problems with court management, like discovery problems generally, were far more likely to be reported by attorneys whose cases were very complex, very contentious, and had very high stakes. Attorneys in complex cases (39% of these attorneys) were more than twice as likely to report court-management problems as were attorneys in cases rated as somewhat complex (19%) or not at all complex (14%). Similarly, attorneys in very contentious cases (43% of attorneys in such cases) were more likely to report court-management problems than were attorneys in cases that were somewhat contentious (24%) or not at all contentious (12%). And finally, attorneys in cases with stakes of $500,000 to $2 million (25% of these attorneys) and in cases with stakes greater than $2 million (36%) were more likely than those in lower-stakes cases (16%) to report problems with court management. There were no meaningful differences by party represented, type of case, or the attorney's level of experience.

Table 33

Percentage of attorneys reporting specific types of court-management problems in cases with some discovery (Question 17*)

Types of court-management problems	($N = 828$)
Discovery planning and implementation problems	13%
Rulings on motions problems	7
Discovery limitations problems	5
Sanctions problems	4

* Refers to the question number in the questionnaire, which can be found at Appendix B.

Although court management was perceived as a problem in some types of cases, this was not generally the case. In fact, as we will discuss further in section IV.12, attorneys in our sample call for increased case management.

11. Is nonuniformity in the disclosure rules a problem?

In examining the issue of nonuniformity, we limited the inquiry to the disclosure rules and distinguished between nonuniformity across districts and nonuniformity within districts. As shown below, there is considerably greater concern about nonuniformity across districts than within districts.

Nonuniformity across districts.

Among attorneys who have an opinion on the issue (30% did not), 60% say moderate to serious problems are created by nonuniform disclosure rules across districts (Table 34). The largest percentage (44%) say the problem is moderate, while 16% rate it as serious. The balance of attorneys (41%) say there is no lack of uniformity or, if there is, it is not a problem.[21] Attorneys who practice in multiple districts are considerably more likely to identify nonuniformity in disclosure as a problem than are attorneys who practice in a smaller number of districts.

Table 34

Percentage of attorneys holding certain opinions regarding the effect of nonuniformity concerning disclosure within a district and across districts (Questions 31 & 32*)

Attorney opinion	Within a district** (N = 949)	Across districts[†] (N = 765)
There is no significant lack of uniformity	47%	13%
Lack of uniformity creates serious problems	6	16
Lack of uniformity creates moderate problems	21	44
Lack of uniformity creates minor or no problems	27	28

* Refers to the question number in the questionnaire, which can be found at Appendix B.

** Responses of "No opinion" (N = 151) and "Other" (N = 17) have been removed.

[†] Responses of "No opinion" (N = 333) and "Other" (N = 20) have been removed.

Nonuniformity within districts.

In contrast to opinions about nonuniformity across districts, relatively few attorneys (6%) think serious problems are created by nonuniform disclosure requirements within the district where the study case was filed. In fact, nearly half the attorneys with an opinion on this issue say there is no significant lack of uniformity in the district.[22]

---

21. Most of those who had no opinion on uniformity across districts said their federal practice takes place primarily in one district (86%). Half of the attorneys who expressed opinions reported practicing in more than one district. The attorneys with no opinion were also far more likely (48% of them) to report that 15% or less of their practice was in federal court than attorneys who expressed opinions (21%). Of the attorneys who expressed opinions on the subject, 76% had more than 15% of their practice in federal court.

22. Also in contrast to the question about uniformity among districts, only 13% of attorneys did not have an opinion on the issue of uniformity within the district where their case was filed.

Coupled with the 27% who say the problem is at most minor, nearly 75% of the attorneys think nonuniformity within a district is not a problem. Anecdote has suggested that attorneys often face a bewildering array of procedural rules within districts. Our findings suggest this is generally not the case for disclosure.

12. If change is necessary, what direction should it take? What changes would be likely to reduce discovery expenses? Should change occur now or later?

We asked attorneys, in several different ways, what changes, if any, should be made in the way discovery is conducted. In the discussion below we focus first on changes aimed at reducing problems and expense in discovery. We then turn to the question of uniformity in the rules—specifically whether uniformity is important and, if so, what form it should take in the case of disclosure.

Changes likely to reduce discovery problems and expenses.

Table 35 sets out thirteen changes that might theoretically reduce discovery expenses. It shows, for both the specific case and cases in general, the percentage of attorneys who said the change would have the desired effect without unreasonably interfering with a fair resolution of the case.

Table 35

Percentage of attorneys with certain opinions about whether specific changes in rules or case-management practice would be likely to reduce expenses without interfering with fair case resolution (Question 18*)

(1) Change in rule or case management practice	(2) Decrease expenses in this case (*N* = 1,036)	(3) Decrease expenses generally		
		All (*N* = 1,036)	Pl. (*N* = 474)	Def. (*N* = 562)
Increasing availability of district or magistrate judges to resolve discovery disputes	18%	54%	55%	53%
Adopting a uniform national rule requiring initial disclosure**	17	44	50	40
Imposing fee-shifting sanctions more frequently and/or imposing more severe sanctions for violations of discovery rules or orders	14	42	41	42
Increasing court management of discovery	13	37	35	39
Adopting a civility code for attorneys	13	42	44	40
Deleting initial disclosure from the national rules	12	31	29	33
Narrowing the definition of what is discoverable (Rule 26(b))**	12	31	22	38
Narrowing the definition of what documents are discoverable (Rule 34)**	11	30	23	37
Limiting—or further limiting—the maximum number of hours for a deposition**	9	27	30	24
Limiting—or further limiting—the time within which to complete discovery	8	19	20	18
Limiting—or further limiting—the number of interrogatories	8	26	27	26
Limiting—or further limiting—the number of depositions	7	23	23	23
Other change	2	5	6	4

* Refers to the question number in the questionnaire, which can be found at Appendix B.

** Differences between plaintiffs' attorneys and defendants' attorneys are statistically significant.

The change most likely to reduce discovery expenses, in the view of our sample of attorneys, is to increase the availability of judges to resolve discovery disputes. Eighteen percent (18%) said that would have helped in the specific case and 54% expect it would help in civil cases generally. The related concept of increasing court management of discovery also ranked high as a means for reducing discovery expenses, with 13% (fourth ranked) saying it would have reduced expenses in the specific case and 37% (fifth ranked) saying it would do so generally.

The second most promising change, both for the specific case and in general, would be a uniform rule requiring disclosure: 17% think it would have helped in the specific case and 44% say this reform would generally serve to reduce discovery expenses. Note that, with regard to the specific case, the 17% saying a uniform rule would have reduced expenses is considerably lower than the 39% who, after experiencing initial disclosure in the case at hand, said it had decreased their client's expenses. We are not sure what explains the discrepancy, though it is possible that a "uniform national rule," as the option was phrased, is not seen as having much effect beyond the effect already achieved by the federal or local provision under which disclosure was required in the sample case.

The third and fourth most-favored changes both involve controls on attorney behavior through more frequent and/or more severe fee-shifting sanctions and through adoption of a civility code for attorneys. For each change, forty-two percent (42%) of the attorneys thought it would reduce expenses generally, while 13–14% said it would have done so in the specific case.

Plaintiffs' attorneys (50% of them) were more likely than defendants' attorneys (40%) to predict cost savings generally from a uniform national rule requiring initial disclosure. Defendants' attorneys, on the other hand, were more likely to predict cost savings from narrowing the scope of discovery, both in general and in relation to document production. This prediction was also more likely to be made by those who practiced in four or more districts and those in firms with ten or more attorneys.

In reading Table 35, a word of caution is in order. Note that for every option, substantially more attorneys predict a general effect (column 3) than would expect there to have been an effect in the specific case (column 2). Consider, for example, Row 3, column 3, which indicates that 31% of the attorneys in our sample think discovery expenses would be reduced by a uniform national rule narrowing the definition of what is discoverable. This should not be taken to mean that those attorneys believe narrowing the scope of discovery will do so in all cases or even in 31% of the cases. One might reasonably read column 3 as predicting that generally there will be a positive effect, namely, that litigation expenses will be reduced without interfering with fair case resolutions.

Column 2, which is based on the experience of attorneys in actual cases, may reflect more realistically the frequency with which the hoped-for effects would materialize. On the other hand, we should keep in mind that the responses in column 2 do not necessarily reflect the extent to which the changes would reduce costs, because for these cases some cost reductions may already have been realized through application of the practices. The actual impact of these practices would likely fall somewhere in between the expectations of column 2 and the predictions of column 3.

The thirteen options listed in Table 35 can be grouped into six broader categories, as they have been in Table 36, which permits us to look at the larger pattern of responses.[23] To reduce discovery expenses, the highest percentage of attorneys would look to increased availability of judges to rule on discovery disputes and/or increased court

---

23. An attorney who checked any item within the group is counted, but a single attorney cannot be counted more than once per group.

management of discovery (63%) and controls on attorney conduct through sanctions and/or a civility code (62%). While substantial numbers would also find certain rule changes helpful—for example, the 44% who said a uniform national rule requiring initial disclosure would reduce expenses and the 35% who said narrowing the scope of discovery would be helpful—changes in judge and attorney behavior clearly outweigh changes in the rules.

A slightly different picture emerges if we combine the responses regarding initial disclosure into a single category. When we do, 71% of the attorneys would find a change in the initial disclosure rules helpful, making this the approach favored by the highest percentage of attorneys. The sentiment is difficult to interpret, however, because the opinions we have combined point in very different directions, one toward requiring initial disclosure universally and the other toward deleting it altogether. While it is tempting to say that the combination points, at least, toward a widespread desire for a uniform rule, we suggest caution in doing so because, while the question about requiring initial disclosure specifically asked about uniformity, the question about deleting it did not. Further insight into attorneys' preferences may be provided, however, by the next two subsections.

Table 36

Percentage of attorneys saying certain types of changes would likely reduce expenses without interfering with fair case resolution (Question 18*)

Types of changes	($N = 1,036$)
Increasing court management/availability of judges to rule on discovery disputes	63%
Increasing sanctions/adopting civility code	62
Numerical limits on time or amount of discovery	45
Adopt a uniform national rule requiring initial disclosure	44
Rule change—scope of discovery	35
Delete initial disclosure from the national rules	31

* Refers to the question number in the questionnaire, which can be found at Appendix B.

The most promising approach to reducing discovery problems.

After presenting the thirteen options above, we asked the attorneys to select the one approach that holds the most promise for reducing discovery problems. The choices focus on three key components of the discovery process: judges, attorneys, and rules of procedure. Of the nearly two-thirds of the attorneys who had an opinion on the subject, about half said judicial case management is the most promising approach to reducing problems in discovery. The remaining half split about equally between revising the rules of civil procedure to further control or regulate discovery or changing client and/or attorney incentives regarding discovery. There were no significant differences in preference by type of party represented in the sample case, number of different discovery problems experienced in the sample case, the type of client the attorney usually represents, type of law practice, or number of years in practice. When pressed to select the single most promising approach to reducing discovery problems, then, the choice that clearly outstrips others is increased judicial case management.

Table 37

Percentage of attorneys selecting each of three approaches as the most promising for reducing discovery problems (Question 19*)

Approach	$(N = 721)$**
Increase judicial case management	47%
Revise the Federal Rules of Civil Procedure to further control or regulate discovery	27
Address the need for changes in client and/or attorney incentives regarding discovery	26

* Refers to the question number in the questionnaire, which can be found at Appendix B.

** Responses of "No opinion" $(N = 208)$ and "Other" $(N = 29)$ have been removed.

Revisions to the discovery rules: the desire for uniform rules.

Apart from the question of whether any changes hold promise for reducing discovery problems, we explored attorneys' preferences about rule changes and uniformity, specifically regarding Rule 26(a)(1). Our questions focused first on the direction change might take and secondly on the timing of any rule revisions.

As to the direction of change, the results are mixed (Table 38). Faced with choice of uniform application of initial disclosure in all districts, uniform absence of initial disclosure, or the status quo, a plurality of attorneys in our sample (41%) support uniform application of initial disclosure. On the other hand, 27% favor a rule with no initial disclosure requirements and a prohibition on local requirements. Setting aside the specific substance of the rule, about two-thirds of attorneys, both plaintiffs and defendants, favor some form of uniform national rule.

Another way to look at the data is to consider the 27% of attorneys who want to delete disclosure and the 30% who favor the status quo (the opt-out system)—in other words, a majority (57%) who prefer something other than a uniform national rule requiring initial disclosure. We must take care, however, not to conclude from this that a majority of attorneys oppose initial disclosure. Such a conclusion would rest on a false assumption that those who favor the status quo disfavor initial disclosure requirements. In fact, 42% of those who favor the status quo are counsel in cases from districts that have implemented initial disclosure. Moreover, more than 40% of those who favor the status quo engaged in initial disclosure in the sample case. For these attorneys, initial disclosure is the status quo. A large proportion of those who favor the status quo, then, have experience with disclosure and do not oppose it (at least not enough to select that choice), but for some reason do not wish to impose a uniform national requirement on districts that have opted out of initial disclosure.

Table 38

Percentage of attorneys with specific preferences regarding types of uniform national rules (Question 33*)

Attorney opinion	All (N = 1,112)	Plaintiffs' attorneys** (N = 504)	Defendants' attorneys** (N = 608)
National rule requiring initial disclosure in every district	41%	45%	38%
National rule with no requirement for initial disclosure and a prohibition on local requirements for initial disclosure	27	22	30
Allowing local districts to decide whether or not to require initial disclosure (status quo)	30	30	30
Other	2	2	2

* Differences between plaintiffs' attorneys' and defendants' attorneys' responses are statistically significant.

** Refers to the question number in the questionnaire, which can be found at Appendix B.

Attorneys who reported use of initial disclosure in the study case were considerably more likely (52% of them) to favor a uniform rule requiring initial disclosure than attorneys who did not report engaging in disclosure (28%) (Table 39). Attorneys who did not use initial disclosure in the sample case were about as likely to favor initial disclosure as to favor prohibition of initial disclosure.

Table 39

Percentage of attorneys preferring certain types of uniform national rules, by participation in initial disclosure (Question 33*)

Attorney opinion	Participation in initial disclosure (N = 503)	No participation in initial disclosure (N = 401)
National rule requiring initial disclosure in every district	52%	28%
National rule with no requirement for initial disclosure and a prohibition on local requirements for initial disclosure	22	31
Allowing local districts to decide whether or not to require initial disclosure (status quo)	23	38
Other	3	2

* Refers to the question number in the questionnaire, which can be found at Appendix B.

Of particular surprise, we found that many attorneys who reported problems with initial disclosure support a uniform national rule requiring disclosure, albeit not in so high a proportion as those experiencing disclosure generally. Of attorneys reporting initial disclosure problems, 47% favored uniform initial disclosure compared to 56% of attorneys who did not report such problems.

We also found that attorneys in cases from districts that had opted out of initial disclosure were somewhat less likely than their counterparts to support a uniform national disclosure rule (35% of these attorneys) and were far more likely to prefer maintenance of the status quo (37%) (Table 40).

Table 40
Percentage of attorneys preferring certain types of uniform national rules, for attorneys in districts opting out and not opting out of initial disclosure (Question 34*)

Attorney opinion	Opt-out ($N = 521$)	No opt-out ($N = 591$)
National rule requiring initial disclosure in every district	35%	47%
National rule with no requirement for initial disclosure and a prohibition on local requirements for initial disclosure	26	27
Allowing local districts to decide whether or not to require initial disclosure (status quo)	37	24
Other	2	3

* Refers to the question number in the questionnaire, which can be found at Appendix B.

Overall, attorneys who represented plaintiffs in the sample cases were more likely to support initial disclosure (45% of them, compared to 38% of defendants' attorneys), while attorneys who represented defendants were more likely to support rules barring initial disclosure (30% of them, compared to 22% of plaintiffs' attorneys) (Table 38). Along similar lines, attorneys who in their overall practice primarily represent plaintiffs (50%) and attorneys who represent plaintiffs and defendants about equally (45%) were more likely than attorneys who primarily represent defendants (34%) to support initial disclosure.

Attorneys' preferences also differed by their practice setting. Solo practitioners (52%) and attorneys in firms of two to ten attorneys (46% of these attorneys) were more likely to support a uniform national disclosure requirement than attorneys in firms of fifty or more attorneys (30%). Attorneys from the largest firms, in turn, were twice as likely to support a prohibition on initial disclosure (39%) than solo practitioners (20%) or attorneys in firms of two to ten attorneys (19%).

These differences might be partially explained by the fact that attorneys in firms of fifty or more attorneys are far more likely to report practicing in four or more districts (45%) than attorneys in firms of two to forty-nine attorneys (18%). Interestingly, though, a plurality of attorneys who practice in four or more districts support initial disclosure (42%) (Table 41). At the same time, these attorneys are more likely (39% of them) than attorneys who practice in fewer districts (21–32%) to support barring initial disclosure rules.

Table 41

Percentage of attorneys preferring certain types of uniform national rules, by number of districts in which they practice* (Question 33**)

Attorney opinion (*N* = 1,105)	1 district	2–3 districts	4 or more districts
National rule requiring initial disclosure in every district	42%	40%	42%
National rule with no requirement for initial disclosure and a prohibition on local requirements for initial disclosure	21	32	39
Allowing local districts to decide whether or not to require initial disclosure (status quo)	35	27	16
Other	3	2	4

* The distributions in this table are statistically significant.

** Refers to the question number in the questionnaire, which can be found at Appendix B.

From our sample of attorneys, the following general picture emerges regarding preferences for the national rules on initial disclosure. Most attorneys prefer a uniform national rule. A plurality of attorneys prefer a rule requiring initial disclosure. This group is disproportionately made up of attorneys who have experience with disclosure, who represent plaintiffs, who practice in a small number of districts, and who practice alone or in small firms. Even so, one would find in this group substantial numbers of other types of attorneys—those who represent defendants, who practice in four or more districts, who practice in large firms, and, surprisingly, who have had problems with initial disclosure.

The timing of rule changes.

While many attorneys favor revisions to the discovery rule, there is a split of opinion about the timing for such revisions (Table 42). A majority favor change in the disclosure rules now, but a substantial minority thinks change should wait until there is more experience with the 1993 changes.

A somewhat clearer picture emerges when we set aside the "No opinion" responses and combine some of the categories. Forty-three percent (43%) of the attorneys in this sample favor immediate changes in the uniformity provisions of the disclosure rules (Item 2 or 3 or both). More broadly, 54% think change of some sort, either in the disclosure rules or other rules, should take place now (Items 2, 3, or 4, or any combination). Finally, the broadest level of support—83% of attorneys—is for some sort of change, either now or later (Items 1, 2, 3, or 4, or any combination).

Table 42

**Percentage of attorneys with various opinions on need for change in
discovery rules at this time* (Question 34**)**

Attorney opinion	($N = 1,101$)
Changes are needed, but should not be considered until we have more experience with recent changes (1)	27%
Changes in uniformity of initial disclosure practices (Rule 26(a)(1)) are needed now (2)	33
Changes in uniformity of expert disclosure practices (Rule 26(a)(2)) are needed now (3)	21
Other changes are needed now (4)	14
No changes are needed (5)	14
No opinion (6)	14

*Because respondents were allowed to choose more than one option, total adds up to more than 100%.

** Refers to the question number in the questionnaire, which can be found at Appendix B.

We found no statistically significant differences regarding the timing of change for plaintiffs versus defendants, by type of primary client, or by numbers of years in practice. Practitioners in four or more federal districts were, however, significantly more likely than others to say that changes in initial disclosure are needed now and significantly less likely to have no opinion (Table 41).

Those who experienced problems with discovery were more likely than those who had no problems to say other changes are needed (Item 4) and were less likely to have no opinion. Similarly, attorneys who experienced problems with initial disclosure were more likely to say changes in initial disclosure, as well as other changes, are needed now. They were also less likely to say they had "No opinion" on the subject.

While it is clear that substantial numbers of attorneys favor further rule changes—and that certain subsets of attorneys in particular favor changing the disclosure rules—it is important to keep in mind that judicial management is viewed by attorneys as the most promising single method for reducing discovery problems (Table 37).

V. Endnote

We began this report by identifying four broad areas of inquiry: (1) the volume and cost of discovery; (2) problems associated with discovery and their cost; (3) the effects of the 1993 amendments; and (4) the need, if any, for rule changes. Our findings about the effects of the 1993 amendments seem relatively straightforward and we see no need to summarize them here. Our discussion of the volume, costs, and problems of discovery, however, warrant attention because they seem to us less clear-cut and definitive.

We found a clear relationship between the volume of discovery activity in a case—as measured by total litigation expenses and discovery expenses—and the monetary stakes in the litigation. That is, as the stakes increase, the volume of discovery, and of discovery problems, also increases. To some extent, then, it appears that the amount of discovery and the frequency of problems is driven simply by the size of the case.

We also identified some case characteristics—the factual complexity of the case as seen by the parties, their rating of the contentiousness of their relationships with the opposing party or counsel, and in some instances the type of case—that appear more often in cases with discovery problems than in other types of cases.

The puzzle that remains is whether these case characteristics have any direct relationship to the volume of discovery and the frequency of discovery problems or whether the size of the case alone explains both volume and the frequency of problems. One plausible hypothesis is that case size alone drives the volume of discovery and that such characteristics as contentiousness are a result of size. Another is that relationships that are already contentious at the outset of the litigation result in cases with large stakes, a high volume of discovery activity, and more discovery problems. Further analysis of our data might yield some answers. Identifying these variables as factors in the equation may help frame the issues for future research.

In any case, the case characteristics revealed by our study—stakes, complexity, contentiousness, and case type—may not help us very much with predicting exactly where the problems might arise, but they may be useful in informing judges and policymakers about what to look for when managing a case or addressing the question of whether to change the rules of civil procedure.

VI. Addendum

After submitting the previous report to the Advisory Committee on Civil Rules at its September 4–5, 1997, meeting at Boston College School of Law, we undertook further analyses using multivariate statistical techniques that, as explained below, permitted a more rigorous examination of relationships among the variables. The following supplemental report was presented to the Advisory Committee at its October 6–7, 1997, meeting:

Summary. We conducted multivariate analyses of variables expected to be correlated with the total cost of litigation or with disposition time. As to total cost, our analyses revealed that cost variables, especially higher monetary stakes, had the strongest relationships with total cost of litigation. The size of the law firm, the type of case, and whether it was complex or contentious were also related to total cost.

As to disposition times, higher monetary stakes and higher levels of complexity were related to a case taking longer, as was billing on an hourly basis. Use of initial disclosure was related to having a shorter disposition time.

Introduction. Our report at Boston College was based primarily on a description of our survey data and a limited number of correlations and cross-tabulations addressing the relationships among two variables (bivariate analysis). We have now had the opportunity to conduct multivariate analyses for the purpose of identifying variables that might be related to two key variables: attorney estimates of the total cost of the litigation and docket data on the time from filing to disposition. Multivariate analyses allow us to look at the relationships between pairs of variables while controlling for the effects of other variables. For example, such analyses permit us to examine whether the number of hours spent in depositions has an independent effect on an outcome measure such as the total cost of the litigation, apart from the impact of, say, the complexity of the case. This memorandum reports the results of these multivariate analyses. For the most part, these analyses confirm results we reported at Boston College.

Two caveats are in order. First, using survey data, which is based on recall, rather than counts of the actual occurrence of events tends to increase the possibility that the analysis will not detect a relationship that actually exists. Second, the analysis does not include all possible variables that might help explain cost or disposition time. For example, criminal caseload in a district may have a great impact on disposition time but is not accounted for in the analysis. Other, often unknown, variables also are not included.

The variables we examine are taken from the survey instrument and from the Center's Integrated Data Base. We classify them as dependent variables (those we are trying to explain) and explanatory variables (those we hypothesize as accounting for time and cost).

Dependent variables

1. Total litigation cost, as measured by attorney estimates; and

2. Disposition time, the time from filing to disposition, as measured by data initially recorded on docket sheets and included in the Center's Integrated Data Base.

Explanatory variables:

1. Cost variables, such as monetary stakes, percentage of cost attributable to particular discovery activities, number of hours spent in depositions, and attorneys' estimates of percentages of total litigation cost due to disclosure and discovery;

2. District initial disclosure policies and whether or not there was initial disclosure and, if so, in what form;

3. Case management by the court, such as presence of a management plan, court conferences to discuss issues;

4. Reported problems with disclosure, discovery, and court management;

5. Attorney characteristics, such as years in practice, firm size, type of clients, and extent of federal practice;

6. Attorney billing method, i.e., hourly or contingency fee basis; and

7. Case characteristics, such as nature of suit, method of disposition, and attorneys' ratings of case complexity and contentiousness.

(1) **Total cost of the litigation.**

To evaluate the impact of various case characteristics on time from filing to disposition, we built a regression model, which is a multivariate statistical technique for identifying which of several potentially explanatory variables best explains variability in the dependent variable. Regression analysis permits us to identify variables that have the strongest relationships with the dependent variable—in this instance, total litigation cost— and to dismiss variables that have weaker or no relationships.

Cost variables: Of the cost variables we examined, we found monetary stakes to be most strongly associated with litigation cost. As stakes increased, overall litigation cost increased. Interestingly, devoting higher <u>percentages</u> of litigation cost to document production was associated with higher total cost, though less strongly than monetary stakes. The number of hours spent in depositions was also associated with increased litigation cost.

District initial disclosure variables were not associated with increased or decreased litigation cost.

Case-management variables were not associated with increased or decreased litigation cost.

Reported problems variables were not associated with increased or decreased litigation cost.

Attorneys' characteristics variables: Of the variables that measured attorney characteristics, we found only one to be related to litigation cost. Costs were higher when the attorney reporting on the case was from a medium-sized firm (11–49 attorneys) or a large firm (50 or more attorneys), compared to smaller firms. This relationship exists independent of other variables, such as case complexity or size of stakes.

Attorney billing method was not associated with increased or decreased litigation cost.

Case characteristics: We found that costs were higher for copyright, patent, and trademark cases and lower for civil rights and contract cases. None of the other case types, such as tort or other federal statutory cases, had a statistically significant relationship to total litigation cost. Costs were higher, however, when the case was contentious or very complex.

In summary, the total cost of litigation is most strongly associated with several other cost variables, especially the size of the monetary stakes. Total cost is also associated with the size of the law firm, the type of case, and whether it was complex or contentious.

(2) <u>Time from filing to disposition.</u>

To examine the time to disposition, we relied on methods drawn from engineering and biostatistics that are now routinely applied to social science issues. Known as survival analysis, these methods can be used to evaluate the impact of explanatory variables on the time from one event to another, here from case filing to disposition. We used survival models to evaluate the relationship between explanatory variables, as identified above, on disposition time.

Cost variables: Of the cost variables, both higher monetary stakes and higher percentages of costs due to depositions were associated with increased time from filing to disposition.

District initial disclosure variables: Disposition time was lower in cases in which initial disclosure was reported to have been used.

Case-management variables were not associated with increases or decreases in disposition times.

Reported problems variables were not associated with increases or decreases in disposition times.

Attorneys' characteristics variables: Curiously, having an attorney who represents both plaintiffs and defendants was associated with decreased disposition times. No other attorney characteristics, including whether the attorney represented a plaintiff or defendant in the case being studied, was associated with disposition time.

Attorney billing method: Attorney reports that they billed on an hourly basis were associated with increased disposition times.

Case characteristics: Longer disposition times also occurred in cases that were moderately or very complex. Shorter disposition times were found in contract, personal property, and civil rights cases.

In summary, the survival model for time to disposition uncovered patterns that were similar, but not identical to, the regression model for total litigation cost. Higher monetary stakes and higher levels of complexity were correlated with a case taking longer. Additionally, in this model initial disclosure is correlated with shorter disposition times and billing on an hourly basis is correlated with longer disposition times.

Appendix A
Methods

Sample size.

Based on an earlier survey of attorneys, we estimated that about 10% of the respondents might identify problems with discovery.[24] Anticipating a response rate of 50%, a sample of 2,000 attorneys would yield about 1,000 responses and approximately 100 problem responses.[25] Therefore, a sample of 1,000 cases was drawn.

As it turned out, the response rate approached 60%,[26] and more than 40% of the attorneys reported some problems with discovery in response to a broad inventory of suggested possible problems. This relatively high rate of identification of problems, however, should not be taken to mean that problems with discovery have increased since the earlier survey. The methods used to identify problems were likely to yield results that are not comparable. In the present study, we sought a comprehensive inventory of problems in four major forms of discovery and we provided a list of potential problems to assist the respondent in identifying such problems, whereas in the previous study, respondents were asked to generate a written response without a list of possible problems.

Population sampled from.

The survey does not purport to cover discovery in all federal civil cases, but instead to cover discovery in general civil litigation in which some discovery activity is reasonably likely. The population of cases sampled from was drawn from all civil cases terminated in the district courts during the last quarter of 1996 (the most recent data then available). For practical reasons we excluded the 8 districts (accounting for 3% of the total district court civil case population) from which we cannot electronically access docket data.[27]

The following types of cases were excluded as not encompassed in the common understanding of general civil litigation or as not likely to involve any discovery: loan collection, prisoner, land condemnation, foreclosure, bankruptcy, drug-related property forfeiture, social security, and asbestos product liability cases (because they are consolidated in an MDL proceeding). We also excluded breast implant cases disposed of in the Northern District of Alabama (about 7% of the total case population for the period) owing to the atypical and highly managed discovery that occurs in mass tort multidistrict

---

24. In the previous survey, about 8% of counsel mentioned discovery problems in written responses to a question asking about the causes of excessive cost or delay in their case. The survey was done as part of the Federal Judicial Center's most recent district court time study.

25. Surveys were sent to 2,016 attorneys; subsequently, sixteen attorneys in nine cases were excluded from the study because they reported that their case was pending.

26. Attorneys returned 1,178 questionnaires. Of those, thirty-one attorneys returned blank surveys indicating that no discovery had occurred in their case. Responses indicating the absence of discovery were entered for those attorneys.

27. These districts may be systematically different from the districts included in the study.

proceedings and because the termination of the cases in the Northern District of Alabama did not represent a final resolution of those cases.

We also excluded all cases that were disposed of by default judgment before issue was joined as well as cases whose termination in the district court is by definition not a final resolution. The latter group was comprised of cases remanded to a state court or to an agency and cases transferred to another district. Finally, we excluded cases that were terminated less than sixty days after their original filing in district court (about 8% of the total case population) on the assumption that very few such cases involve any discovery.

Overall, the population sampled from accounts for about 45% of civil cases filed in the district courts. That is, cases excluded from consideration account for about 55%.

Representativeness of the responses.

In the sample cases, 47% of the attorneys represented plaintiffs[28] and 53% represented defendants, including third-party defendants. Among those who responded, 46% represented plaintiffs and 54% represented defendants. We also asked respondents what types of clients they generally represent and found that 28% represent primarily plaintiffs, 44% represent primarily defendants, and 27% represent plaintiffs and defendants about equally. We present data separately for attorneys for plaintiffs and defendants—based on the client represented in the sample case—when there are notable differences in their responses.

Responding attorneys, on the average, devoted 41% (median = 30%) of their work time during the past five years to federal civil litigation. The majority (51%) practice primarily in one federal district, but 39% practice in two or three federal districts and 10% practice in four or more federal districts.

The majority practice in firms of two to forty-nine attorneys; 20% are from firms of fifty or more attorneys; 12% are sole practitioners; and 8% are government attorneys. On the average, these attorneys have practiced law for sixteen years; 75% have practiced law for at least ten years.

We compared the cases underlying the responses with the cases in the original sample and found the responses to be representative of the sample as a whole. We found little or no difference between the original set of cases and the subset of cases in which responding attorneys were counsel. In both sets, the types of cases and their life spans (from filing to disposition) showed no substantial differences, and the methods of disposition, whether by trial, settlement, motion, or otherwise were substantially equivalent.

We specifically examined the disclosure rules in place in various districts in the sample. Response rates were almost identical from districts with initial disclosure and from those without initial disclosure and from district with variations of disclosure and nondisclosure.

---

28. The sample included a number of pro se plaintiffs and a smaller number of pro se defendants. In selecting the sample cases, we tried not to include those with pro se parties. Nonetheless, some made it into the sample. However, responses from pro se parties are not included in the analysis reported here.

<u>Data analysis</u>.

At the preliminary stage of analysis reported in section IV, data analysis is generally based on cross-tabulations of the data and comparison of responses using a chi-square test of differences between pairs of variables. Occasionally, where noted in the text, we have used the Pearson correlation coefficient to examine relationships among variables. Later analyses, reported in the Addendum, section VI, are based on two multivariate statistical techniques, multiple regression and survival analysis.

Appendix B

National Survey of Counsel re Disclosure and Discovery Practice in Closed Federal Civil Cases

For the Advisory Committee on Civil Rules of the Judicial Conference of the United States

Designed and administered by the Federal Judicial Center

Who Should Complete the Questionnaire?

Court records show that you represented a party in a recently terminated case identified in the cover letter ("the named case"). We ask that the questionnaire be completed by the primary attorney (or attorneys) who represented your client or clients in this case. If that is someone other than yourself, please pass this questionnaire along to the appropriate attorney. If the attorney primarily responsible for this case is no longer available, please return the questionnaire with a note to that effect. We are sending an identical questionnaire to attorneys for other parties in the litigation.

Origin and Purpose

This questionnaire was designed by the Federal Judicial Center at the request of the Judicial Conference's Civil Rules Advisory Committee. The Federal Judicial Center is the research arm for the federal judiciary. The Civil Rules Advisory Committee drafts and recommends changes in the Federal Rules of Civil Procedure pursuant to the Rules Enabling Act, 28 U.S.C. §§ 2071-2077. This research is being conducted by the Federal Judicial Center to assist the Advisory Committee in its current examination of discovery rules.

Confidentiality

All information that would permit identification of the named case, the lawyers, or the parties is strictly confidential. Findings will be reported in the aggregate so no individual person or case will be identifiable. The code number on the back of the questionnaire will be used only to link information from this questionnaire to information we have about the case from court records and to communicate further with you.

Results

If you would like a summary of the results, please check this box:❏

Returning the Questionnaire

Please return the questionnaire in the enclosed envelope by **June 13, 1997**. If you have questions or would like to discuss the questionnaire, please call Tom Willging or John Shapard at 202-273-4070.

Part I: Discovery Activity in the Named Case. *Please answer the questions in Part I with reference to the named case only.*

Discovery planning.

1. Did you, or other counsel for your client, meet and confer with opposing counsel, by telephone, correspondence, or in person, to plan for discovery, in accordance with Fed. R. Civ. P. 26(f) or a similar local rule, order, or other provision? *Note: The subscripts after each response box are for our use in entering the data accurately.*

   Please check one: ❏$_1$ Yes

                        ❏$_2$ No--------------------------------> *go to question 3.*

                        ❏$_3$ I don't recall -------------------> *go to question 3.*

2. *Note that this question and a number of later questions ask about your client's litigation expenses. As to all such questions, if your client was not charged attorneys' fees on a standard hourly basis, please answer in light of what fees would likely have been if charged at a standard hourly rate.*

   What effects did meeting and conferring to plan for discovery have on the following aspects of the named case?

   Please circle one number in each row:

Effect of meeting and conferring on	Increased	Had no effect	Decreased	I can't say
Your client's overall litigation expenses$_1$	1	2	3	4
Time from filing to disposition$_2$	1	2	3	4
Overall procedural fairness$_3$	1	2	3	4
Fairness of case outcome$_4$	1	2	3	4
Number of issues$_5$	1	2	3	4

   Please note any other positive or negative aspects of meeting and conferring to plan for discovery in this case:

   _____

   _____

   _____

3. Was there a plan for discovery, either as a stand-alone plan or as part of a scheduling order?

   Please check one: ❏$_1$ Yes

                            ❏$_2$ No

                            ❏$_3$ I don't recall

Informal exchange of discoverable information.

4. Apart from the requirements of the federal rules or local provisions, did you, or other counsel for your client, voluntarily provide or receive discoverable information informally in the named case?

    Please check one: ❏₁ Yes

                  ❏₂ No

                  ❏₃ I don't recall

If there was neither discovery of any type nor initial disclosure of information identified in Fed. R. Civ. P. 26(a)(1), (as defined in question 5), or a similar local provision, go to question 18, column 2 (page 9). Otherwise, proceed to question 5, below.

Initial disclosure.

5. Fed. R. Civ. P. 26(a)(1) or similar local provisions in some districts require litigants to provide descriptions or lists of witnesses, documents, data compilations, damage computations, insurance agreements, or other tangible materials. Did you, or other counsel for your client, provide or receive initial disclosure in this case?

    Please check one: ❏₁ Yes

                        ❏₂ No ----------------------> *go to question 8.*

                        ❏₃ I don't recall ----------> *go to question 9.*

6. Which of the following statements describe the initial disclosure that took place?

    Please check all that apply:

         ❏₁ My client disclosed lists or descriptions of documents and/or materials.

         ❏₂ My client disclosed copies of documents and/or materials.

         ❏₃ My client received lists or descriptions of documents and/or materials.

         ❏₄ My client received copies of documents and/or materials.

         ❏₅ I don't recall.

7. What effects did initial disclosure have on the named case?

   Please circle one number in each row:

Effect of initial disclosure on	Increased	Had no effect	Decreased	I can't say
Your client's overall litigation expenses$_1$	1	2	3	4
Time from filing to disposition$_2$	1	2	3	4
Overall procedural fairness$_3$	1	2	3	4
Fairness of case outcome$_4$	1	2	3	4
Prospects of settlement$_5$	1	2	3	4
Amount of discovery$_6$	1	2	3	4
Number of discovery disputes$_7$	1	2	3	4

Please note any other positive or negative aspects of initial disclosure in this case:

_____

_____

_____

PLEASE GO TO QUESTION 9.

Reason for lack of initial disclosure. *To be answered only by those who answered "No" to question 5.*

8. Why was there no initial disclosure in this case?

   Please check all that apply:

   ❏$_1$ The district exempted all cases from initial disclosure.

   ❏$_2$ The district exempted this type of case from initial disclosure.

   ❏$_3$ The judge assigned to this case has a standing order exempting all cases from initial disclosure.

   ❏$_4$ The judge assigned to this case exempted this case from initial disclosure.

   ❏$_5$ The parties stipulated that disclosure provisions would not apply to this case.

   ❏$_6$ No one began the process and the court did not take action to enforce disclosure requirements.

   ❏$_7$ Other (specify) _____

   ❏$_8$ I don't know.

Expert discovery and disclosure.

9. Did you, or another attorney for your client, do any of the following regarding expert witnesses?

Please check all that apply:

❏₁ Provide, pursuant to Fed. R. Civ. P. 26(a)(2) or a similar local provision, a written expert report (not just a list of the experts)

❏₂ Receive, pursuant to Fed. R. Civ. P. 26(a)(2) or a similar local provision, another party's written expert report (not just a list of the experts)

❏₃ Agree with an opposing party not to disclose written reports of anticipated expert testimony

❏₄ Attend or conduct the deposition of an expert

❏₅ Conduct other expert discovery (please specify): _____

❏₆ None of the above

❏₇ I don't recall

10. Regardless of whether disclosure occurred in this case, if expert disclosure was or would have been required by Fed. R. Civ. P. 26(a)(2) or a similar local provision, what effects did that requirement have?

If expert disclosure was not required or would not have been required, go to question 11.

Please circle one number in each row:

Effect of expert disclosure requirement on	Increased	Had no effect	Decreased	I can't say
Your client's overall litigation expenses₁	1	2	3	4
Time from filing to disposition₂	1	2	3	4
Overall procedural fairness₃	1	2	3	4
Fairness of case outcome₄	1	2	3	4
Pressure to settle₅	1	2	3	4

Please note any other positive or negative aspects of expert discovery in this case:

_____

_____

_____

_____

<u>Types of discovery</u>.

11. If you, or another attorney for your client, conducted, defended, or attended a deposition by oral examination, what was

         11a. the estimated number of individuals deposed?   _____ deponents

         11b. the estimated total hours spent in those depositions?   _____ hours

         11c. the estimated length of the longest deposition?   _____ hours

12. Aside from oral depositions or initial disclosure, what other types of discovery were used in this case?

    Please check <u>all that apply</u>:

      ❏₁ Interrogatories

      ❏₂ Requests for production of documents

      ❏₃ Requests for admissions

      ❏₄ Physical or mental examination

      ❏₅ Other (please specify): _____

      ❏₆ I can't recall

<u>Problems in disclosure or discovery</u>.

13. Please indicate which, if any, of the following types of problems occurred in the named case in relation to any party in the case.

Please check <u>all that apply</u>:

 ❏$_1$ There were no problems with disclosure or discovery--------------> *go to question 16.*

Initial disclosure

❏$_1$ Disclosure was too brief or incomplete.
❏$_2$ Disclosure was excessive.
 ❏$_3$ Some disclosed materials were also requested in discovery.
 ❏$_4$ A party failed to supplement or update the disclosures.
 ❏$_5$ A party disclosed required information and another party did not disclose required information.
 ❏$_6$ Disclosure occurred only after a motion to compel or an order from the court.
 ❏$_7$ Sanctions were imposed for failure to disclose.
 ❏$_8$ Other (please specify): _____

Document production

❏$_1$ One or more requests were vague.
❏$_2$ An excessive number of documents were requested.
❏$_3$ Materials provided were excessive or disordered.
❏$_4$ A party failed to respond in a timely fashion.
❏$_5$ A party failed to respond adequately.
 ❏$_6$ Other (please specify):

_____

Oral depositions

❏$_1$ There were too many depositions.
❏$_2$ Too much time was taken in some or all depositions.
❏$_3$ An attorney coached a witness during a deposition.
❏$_4$ An attorney improperly instructed a witness not to answer a question.
 ❏$_5$ An attorney acted unreasonably to annoy, embarrass, or oppress the deponent or counsel.
❏$_6$ Other (please specify): _____

Expert Disclosure

❏$_1$ Expert disclosure was too brief or incomplete.
❏$_2$ Expert disclosure was too expensive.
 ❏$_3$ A party failed to supplement or update its disclosures.
 ❏$_4$ Other (please specify):

_____

Other Problems

 ❏$_1$ Please identify any other problems with disclosure or discovery: _____

_____

_____

14. Please estimate the <u>percentage</u> of your client's <u>discovery expenses</u> that were incurred unnecessarily because of these problems:

_____ %

15. To what extent did each of the following factors contribute to any problems in discovery in relation to any party?

Please circle <u>one number in each row</u>:

Factor	No contribution	Moderate contribution	Major contribution	I can't say
Intentional delays or complications$_1$	1	2	3	4
Lack of cooperation by a client$_2$	1	2	3	4
Pursuit of discovery disproportionate to the needs of the case$_3$	1	2	3	4
Incompetence or inexperience of counsel$_4$	1	2	3	4

Please identify any other factors that may have contributed to discovery problems in this case: _____

_____

_____

<u>Court management of discovery</u>.

16. Did the court do any of the following in this case?

Please check <u>all that apply</u>:

❏$_1$ Hold a conference (by telephone, correspondence, or in person) to consider a discovery plan

❏$_2$ Hold a conference at which discovery issues (other than a discovery plan) were discussed

❏$_3$ Limit the time for completion of discovery? If so, to how many months? _____ months

❏$_4$ Enforce the federal rules' limits on the number of interrogatories or depositions

❏$_5$ Limit the number of interrogatories or depositions to fewer than specified in the federal rules

❏$_6$ Increase the number of interrogatories or depositions to more than specified in the federal rules

❏$_7$ Rule on a discovery motion

❏$_8$ None of the above

17. Please indicate whether any of the following problems occurred regarding the court's management of discovery in relation to any party.

    Please check all that apply:

    $\square_1$ There were no problems with the court's management
    of disclosure or discovery --> *go to question 18*

Discovery planning and implementation

$\square_1$ There were no time limits on discovery and such limits were needed.
$\square_2$ The time allowed for discovery was too long.
$\square_3$ The time allowed for discovery was too short.
$\square_4$ The court allowed too many extensions of the deadline to complete discovery.
$\square_5$ The court allowed too many extensions of time to respond to discovery requests.
$\square_6$ The court was too rigid about deadlines.
$\square_7$ Other (please specify): _____

Limitations on discovery

$\square_1$ There were no limits on interrogatories and such limits were needed.
$\square_2$ There were no limits on depositions and such limits were needed.
$\square_3$ Limits on interrogatories were too lenient.
$\square_4$ Limits on interrogatories were too restrictive.
$\square_5$ Limits on depositions were too lenient.
$\square_6$ Limits on depositions were too restrictive.
$\square_7$ Other (please specify): _____

Rulings on motions

$\square_1$ There was no decisionmaker available to rule on disputes during depositions.
$\square_2$ Rulings on discovery motions took too long.
$\square_3$ There were no rulings on discovery motions and such rulings were needed.
$\square_4$ Other (please specify): _____

Sanctions

$\square_1$ There were no rulings on sanctions motions and such rulings were needed.
$\square_2$ Rulings on sanctions motions took too long.
$\square_3$ Rulings on sanctions motions were generally too lenient.
$\square_4$ Rulings on sanctions motions were generally too harsh.
$\square_5$ Other (please specify): _____

Other problems

$\square_1$ Please identify any other problems with the court's management of discovery in this case: ____

_____

_____

Changes in rules or case management practices.

18. Which of the following types of changes in the Federal Rules of Civil Procedure or court management practices would be likely to have reduced discovery expenses **either in this case or generally**, without unreasonably interfering with the fair resolution of this case or most cases?

Please circle all that apply:

Change in rule or case management practice	(Column 1) Would have been likely to decrease expenses in this case without unreasonably interfering with fair resolution	(Column 2) Would generally be likely to decrease expenses without unreasonably interfering with fair resolutions
Adopting a uniform national rule requiring initial disclosure[1]	1	2
Deleting initial disclosure from the national rules[2]	1	2
Narrowing the definition of what is discoverable (Rule 26(b))[3]	1	2
Narrowing the definition of what documents are discoverable (Rule 34)[4]	1	2
Limiting—or further limiting—the time within which to complete discovery[5]	1	2
Limiting—or further limiting—the number of depositions[6]	1	2
Limiting—or further limiting—the maximum number of hours for a deposition[7]	1	2
Limiting—or further limiting—the number of interrogatories[8]	1	2
Increasing court management of discovery[9]	1	2
Increasing availability of district or magistrate judges to resolve discovery disputes[10]	1	2
Imposing fee-shifting sanctions more frequently and/or imposing more severe sanctions for violations of discovery rules or orders[11]	1	2
Adopting a civility code for attorneys[12]	1	2
Other change (specify)[13] _____	1	2

19. In considering changes to civil rules regarding discovery, discovery case management practices, or other reforms, which of the following approaches holds the most promise for reducing any problems in discovery?

Please check one:

❏[1] Revise the Federal Rules of Civil Procedure to further control or regulate discovery

❏[2] Increase judicial case management

❏[3] Address the need for changes in client and/or attorney incentives regarding discovery

❏[4] Other (please specify): _____

❏[5] No opinion

Expenses of this litigation.

20. Please estimate the total litigation expenses for your client in this case, including such items as expert witness fees, transcript fees, litigation support fees, and fees for attorneys and paralegals, but excluding any expenses relating to appeals. *If your client was not charged attorneys' fees on a standard hourly basis, please answer the following questions in light of what fees would likely have been if charged at a standard hourly rate.*

$ _____

21. Approximately what percentage of the total litigation expenses for your client were associated with disclosure and discovery activity?

_____ % of the total litigation expenses

22. Please indicate the approximate percentage of total discovery expenses allocable to each of these types of discovery. Fair estimates from your recollection are satisfactory, but the estimates should add up to 100%. Include estimates of the expenses of motions activity in the categories to which the motion pertained.

_____$_1$% Meet and confer/discovery planning

_____$_2$% Initial disclosure of documents and materials by rule or order, or voluntarily

_____$_3$% Expert disclosure or discovery

_____$_4$% Depositions

_____$_5$% Requests for and/or production of documents not disclosed at any initial disclosure

_____$_6$% Interrogatories

_____$_7$% Other (please describe):

_____

  100 % Total

Stakes in the case.

23. Aside from the expenses of litigation, what specific relief was at stake for your client in this case? If possible, estimate and include the monetary value of any nonmonetary relief at stake.

23a. The dollar value of the worst likely outcome, including damages, monetary relief and quantifiable nonmonetary relief, was that my client would

❑$_1$ gain or ❑$_2$ lose $_____

23b. The dollar value of the best likely outcome, including damages, monetary relief and quantifiable nonmonetary relief, was that my client would

❑$_1$ gain or ❑$_2$ lose $_____

24. To what extent was your client concerned about nonmonetary relief that was not quantified above or about possible consequences beyond the relief sought in this specific case, such as future litigation based on similar claims, legal precedent, harm to reputation, or a desire to maintain a business relationship with a party?

Please check one:
- ❏₁ Such consequences were of dominant concern to my client.
- ❏₂ Such consequences were of some concern to my client.
- ❏₃ Such consequences were of little or no concern to my client.
- ❏₄ I can't say.

Attorneys' fees.

25. What was your arrangement with your client regarding attorneys' fees in this case?

Please check all that apply:
- ❏₁ Hourly billings
- ❏₂ Contingent fee (percentage of recovery)
- ❏₃ Other arrangement not based on hours or case outcome
- ❏₄ I can't say

26. Was there a statutory provision for recovery of attorneys' fees applicable to this case?

Please check one:
- ❏₁ Yes
- ❏₂ No
- ❏₃ I don't recall

Complexity.

27. How complex were the factual issues in this case?

Please check one:
- ❏₁ Very complex
- ❏₂ Somewhat complex
- ❏₃ Not at all complex
- ❏₄ I don't recall

Contentiousness.

28. Overall, how contentious were the relationships among opposing attorneys and clients in this case?

Please check one:
- ❏₁ Very contentious
- ❏₂ Somewhat contentious
- ❏₃ Not at all contentious
- ❏₄ I don't recall

Summary assessment.

29. On the whole, did the disclosure and discovery generated by all parties in this case amount to too much, too little, or about the right amount of the information needed for a fair resolution of this case?

Please check one: ❏₁ Too much

❏₂ About right

❏₃ Too little

❏₄ No opinion

30. On the whole, was the cost of disclosure and discovery in this case high, low, or about right relative to your client's stakes in this case?

Please check one: ❏₁ High

❏₂ About right

❏₃ Low

❏₄ No opinion

Part II. Opinions Based on Personal Experiences. *For the questions in this section, you need not limit your responses to the experiences gained in the case identified earlier in the survey, but please draw only upon experiences with your own federal cases.*

Uniformity.

31. How serious is the lack of uniformity, if any, in practices among district judges in the district in which the named case was filed in regard to disclosure activity?

Please check all that apply:

❏₁ In my experience, there is no significant lack of uniformity in that district.

❏₂ The lack of uniformity in that district creates serious problems.

❏₃ The lack of uniformity in that district creates moderate problems.

❏₄ The lack of uniformity in that district creates minor problems or no problems.

❏₅ Other (please explain): _____

❏₆ No opinion

32. How serious is the lack of uniformity, if any, in practices among districts in regard to disclosure activity?

Please check all that apply:

❏₁ In my experience, there is no significant lack of uniformity among districts.

❏₂ The lack of uniformity among districts creates serious problems.

❏₃ The lack of uniformity among districts creates moderate problems.

❏₄ The lack of uniformity among districts creates minor problems or no problems.

❏₅ Other (please explain): _____

❏₆ No opinion

33. Some have asserted that uniform national rules should be adopted regarding initial disclosure under Fed. R. Civ. P. 26(a)(1). Which of the following proposed types of uniform national rules do you prefer?

    Please check one:

    ❏₁ A national rule requiring initial disclosure in every district

    ❏₂ A national rule with no requirement for initial disclosure and a prohibition on local requirements for initial disclosure

    ❏₃ Allowing local districts to decide whether or not to require initial disclosure (the status quo)

    ❏₄ Other (please explain): _____

Changes in discovery rules.

34. What is your opinion regarding the need for change in the discovery rules at this time?

    Please check all that apply:

    ❏₁ Changes are needed, but should not be considered until we have more experience with recent changes.

    ❏₂ Changes in uniformity of initial disclosure practices (Rule 26(a)(1)) are needed now.

    ❏₃ Changes in uniformity of expert disclosure practices (Rule 26(a)(2)) are needed now.

    ❏₄ Other changes are needed now. Please identify: _____

    ❏₅ No changes are needed.

    ❏₆ No opinion

Part III. Nature of Law Practice.

35. Which of the following best describes your law practice setting?

    Please check one: ❏₁ Sole practitioner

    ❏₂ Private firm of 2-10 lawyers

    ❏₃ Private firm of 11-49 lawyers

    ❏₄ Private firm of 50 or more lawyers

    ❏₅ Legal staff of a for-profit corporation or entity

    ❏₆ Legal staff of a non-profit corporation or entity

    ❏₇ Government

    ❏₈ Other (please specify):

    _____

36. How many years have you been engaged in the practice of law? _____ years

37. What types of clients do you generally represent?

    Please check one: ❏₁ Primarily plaintiffs

    ❏₂ Primarily defendants

    ❏₃ Plaintiffs and defendants about equally

    ❏₄ Other (specify): _____

38. What percentage of your work time has been devoted to federal civil litigation during the past five years (or during the time you have been in practice, if less than five years)?

_____ % of my work time

39. In how many federal districts does your federal practice primarily take place?

Please check one: ❏₁ Primarily in 1 federal district

❏₂ Primarily in 2 or 3 federal districts

❏₃ In 4 or more federal districts

40. Comments. *Please add any comments you may have about your experiences with discovery or disclosure generally.*